THE SKILL OF HAPPINESS

Creating Daily Ecstasy With Vivation

What They Are Saying...

"Vivation is what you've been looking for. By using the simple process of Vivation, you can eliminate your problems and give yourself the life you truly want in your heart. You can renew the sense of wonder and excitement you only vaguely remember. You can once again have fun and enjoy life. The only way you'll know the wonders that await you is to try Vivation yourself. The book you hold in your hands is your ticket to a new life. It's high time every person on Earth, especially our troubled leaders, experienced daily ecstasy. Vivation is the way."
—**Victor Boc**, from the Introduction

"Transformational personal growth is an essential element in a happy, successful life. Vivation is the most powerful transformational process I have ever experienced. I enthusiastically recommend Jim Leonard's work to everyone."
—**Dick Bertram**, Founder of Bertram Yachts

"Vivation has had a profound effect on my life and my happiness. As an astrologer, I am constantly recommending the practice to clients who feel powerless over negative relationship patterns, confidence problems, and self-worth issues. Thank God for Jim Leonard's work."
—**James Braha**, author, *Ancient Hindu Astrology for the Modern Western Astrologer*

"Vivation is a powerful skill for clearing and integrating feelings and increasing psychospiritual awareness. I highly recommend it!"
—**Steven Farmer**, psychotherapist and author, *The Wounded Male* and *Adult Children of Abusive Parents*

THE SKILL OF HAPPINESS

Creating Daily Ecstasy With Vivation

JIM LEONARD

THREE BLUE HERONS PUBLISHING, INC.

THE SKILL OF HAPPINESS

Creating Daily Ecstasy With Vivation

JIM LEONARD

This book is intended for entertainment purposes only. Vivation is an experimental meditation and its effect (if any) on pre-existing or latent pathological mental or physical conditions is unknown. No claims are made about any specific results that one might receive from this program. Vivation is a self-directed self-improvement process and all results that one gets from doing Vivation are created only by that person. No warranty is made for any results that the reader might obtain, or not obtain, by trying anything described herein.

ISBN 1-881952-09-6

Cover art by Wisconsin artist *ZAK*

THREE BLUE HERONS PUB., INC.
PO Box 463
Fond du Lac, Wisconsin 54936-0463
Tel.: 414-921-6991 Fax: 414-921-7691

ACKNOWLEDGMENTS

Lans Peterson for editing, for helping me refine my ability to teach Vivation, and for being sweet to me while I wrote this book.

Victor Boc for being a terrific editor and for being my pal for fifteen years. Thanks for the great introduction, too!

Patrizia Terreno for convincing me to write this book.

Dr. Anthony S. Dallmann-Jones for editorial assistance, and for having the courage, wisdom, and vision to publish this book.

All of my friends, students and colleagues in the world-wide Vivation Community. I couldn't have done it without you.

To all who are willing...

THE SKILL OF HAPPINESS

Creating Daily Ecstasy With Vivation

TABLE OF CONTENTS

INTRODUCTION

by Victor Boc

Author, *How To Solve All Your Money Problems Forever*

If you are fortunate enough to meet Jim Leonard you will notice immediately that he is no ordinary human being. Jim radiates happiness—as if he's found some sort of inner tranquillity that cannot be disturbed. He has laughing eyes. He laughs easily and often, not only at jokes, but even in the face adversity. He seems to have fun all the time.

Jim Leonard has perfected a process which is having a major impact on the world as we know it. He has devoted his life to learning about this process and teaching it to others. Future generations will look back with admiration and gratitude to this man who walks in our midst today, this man who gave the world Vivation.

In the 1970's and 80's, I hosted a radio talk show in the San Francisco Bay Area of California. I focused my program on topics of personal growth. Over the years, hundreds of guests appeared on my show pushing their various techniques for self-improvement. Since many of them gave me complimentary "samples" of what they had to offer, I was able to try dozens of seminars and courses. I experienced bodywork, meditation, self-hypnosis and every hot new workshop of the day. I found most of these practices to have something of value, but Vivation was, without question, unlike anything else. Vivation was definitely in a class by itself.

To me, Vivation was the only technique that *really did something*, the only one that consisted of nothing but pure experience. In all other practices, someone sat me down and told me stuff, talked to me and told me what to do. Vivation was different. Nobody directed me and told me what to think and feel. The experience was mine alone, nonverbal but real. Vivation was unlike anything I'd ever experienced before. It was great. It blew my mind! And I've never been the same since.

Vivation has made an immense difference in my life. Vivation is the one process, of all those I tried, that truly changed me inside, to the core. My relationships with other people, particularly my mother, changed instantly and dramatically. My creativity and ability to act decisively improved tremendously. I experienced relaxation and peace of mind, based on a direct knowledge of the life-force within. I know for certain that I am healthier and happier today than had I never learned Vivation. In fact, the way my life was going, I honestly wonder whether I'd even be alive now were it not for Vivation.

Vivation is what you've been looking for. By using the simple process of Vivation, you can eliminate your problems and give yourself the life you truly want in your heart. You can renew the sense of wonder and excitement you vaguely remember in distant memory. You can once again have fun and enjoy life. The only way you'll know the wonders that await you is to try Vivation yourself.

The book you hold in your hands is your ticket to a new life. It's high time every person on Earth, especially our troubled leaders, experienced daily ecstasy. Vivation is the way.

Have fun with it!

Victor Boc
March, 1996
Eugene, Oregon

CHAPTER 1

WHAT VIVATION WILL DO FOR YOU

How are Swedes like Africans? What do Russians share in common with Australians, and Brazilians share in common with Japanese? What unites Jews, Christians, Moslems, Buddhists and atheists? What do doctors, jazz drummers, Air Force Colonels, hairdressers, and sheriff's deputies all have in common? How is a man who wants to quit smoking like a woman who wants to open her own business?

All these people, and tens of thousands more, are using Vivation*, right now, to increase their happiness, effectiveness, and creativity.

Vivation is a process for harmonizing the emotional and spiritual energies of the body. Vivation can be applied in dedicated sessions and also in day-to-day life, during both pleasant and unpleasant experiences. When you are dealing with something difficult, Vivation relaxes you into a more creative perspective and frees you from whatever negativity was keeping you stuck. When experiencing pleasurable situations and feelings, it allows you to be more present and receptive.

[*The word *Vivation* is derived from the Latin word for *life*. It means the process of embracing life fully.]

Vivation makes every kind of change easier by facilitating an appropriate response and internal harmony. Vivation is the skill of happiness. Vivation enables you to produce superior outcomes by removing negative factors from your own subconscious. Yet Vivation works at the feeling level—it is not a mental process.

Specifically, Vivation causes *integration*. Integration means experiencing a feeling honestly and embracing it fully. Integration is the opposite of *suppression*. When you hide from a feeling or try to make it go away, you suppress it. When you face the feeling squarely and accept it, you integrate it.

Integration is physical as well as mental. Emotions are made of energy—energy you can use constructively. However, until you integrate an emotion, you hold its energy away as though it were separate from you. Once you integrate the emotion, its energy merges back into your overall aliveness. In the same moment, you gain the lesson the emotion has for you.

Every integration is a quantum leap in receptivity to the benefits, pleasures and learning available from something in your life. Each integration invites your body to present you with the next feeling. As you develop skill with the technique you can cause many integrations very quickly, and in each session you experience a healing adventure into the depths of yourself.

Often you will hear people say to you, "Be here now," or "You just need to love yourself," but they never tell you *how* to do these things. That's where Vivation comes in. The Vivation session goes beyond healing the past—it connects you with your ecstatic essence in the present. Vivation is the skill of loving yourself exactly as you are.

Nothing facilitates change as well as being at peace with the present moment. You are never infinitely far from any goal. It is always easier to achieve any goal when you focus on your nearness to the goal rather than on your distance from the goal. Vivation makes this shift to empowerment and enthusiasm at a level much deeper than the mind—it goes right to the cells of your body and the depth of your being.

Just below the threshold of your normal awareness lies an entire universe of memories, imaginings, and longings. This hidden world is a realm you sometimes remember as you awaken from sleep. It has landscapes as vast, and treasures as brilliant as any you'll find in the ordinary world, yet most people scarcely glimpse this realm in an entire lifetime. Vivation takes you on a journey into this inner world. Your breath and your feeling sense give you wings.

The breathing you use in Vivation is called Circular Breathing. It is continuous, without pauses. The inhale is intentional and the exhale is relaxed. Circular Breathing creates waves of energy in your body that you can readily feel. The waves of energy massage and caress you from the inside. Simultaneously, the waves carry valuable information to you from your subconscious.

Vivation is more than Circular Breathing. When you learn Vivation you learn how to create the physical energy of unconditional love within yourself. As feelings and emotions arise during the process, you feel them in detail and embrace them. Your unconditional love, even more than the breathing itself, creates the results.

A proverb says, "If you give a man a fish, you feed him for a day. If you teach him how to fish, you feed him for a lifetime." In Vivation we do more than lead you through a profound healing experience, we teach you how to cause the experience for yourself. Every session is both a deep experience of loving yourself and a lesson in how to be more loving with yourself forever.

At first you learn Vivation from a trained teacher, your Vivation Professional. After just a few lessons you can learn to give yourself complete Vivation sessions whenever and wherever you wish. Each Vivation session gives you profound insight into yourself and deep healing of energy blockages and emotional scars. When you complete your session, you feel refreshed and revitalized.

You can also do Vivation while engaging in other activities. This is called "Vivation in Action". Vivation in Action enables you to be more present with whatever is going on, less emotionally reactive, and more centered and creative. When you do Vivation in Action in the presence of other people, no one will detect that you are doing anything unusual. Instead it will only strike them that you are a particularly cheerful and centered individual.

Since I developed Vivation in 1979, I have personally facilitated more than 30,000 Vivation sessions in twenty countries. I have therefore had ample opportunity to observe the results people get from doing Vivation. Obviously different people have different situations in their lives. Therefore the results people get from doing Vivation are as varied as people themselves. However, I have observed certain consistent benefits obtained by nearly everyone who learns Vivation. The following are some of the ways *you* can use Vivation:

Use Vivation to Reduce Stress

Vivation is a stress reduction technique so effective that the stress never comes back! Integration of emotions is permanent. Vivation uses breathing to make a connection between your suppressed emotions and your spiritual essence. At the same time that it eliminates worry and negativity, it relaxes you and renews you physically.

One woman recently told me that before she started Vivation she had terrible anxiety every time her husband worked at night and she remained home alone. After a few Vivation sessions she noticed she didn't have the fear anymore.

If you want to reduce stress, Vivation is the best way to start your day. Take a few minutes to Vive instead of rushing immediately to the coffee pot. Vivation reduces the perceived need for caffeine or other stimulants, which contribute to stress. An additional benefit to starting your day with Vivation is that interesting feelings are often left over from dreams. These feelings can be explored and integrated to produce lasting benefits.

Vivation is also an excellent way to end the day and prepare for restful sleep. Meditating on the subtle changes that happen from moment to moment in your feelings quiets the mind and makes you less mental. Vivation relaxes your muscles. A pulse of relaxation passes through your entire body with each breath. Vivation is very much like giving yourself a massage from the inside.

Stress is caused by an excess of controlling impulses in the nervous system, the "fight or flight" mechanism. Vivation provides the creative breakthroughs that help you see the best ways to proceed with getting what you want, while letting go of the impulse to beat down obstacles with your will.

Vivation also makes the best possible break between your work life and your personal life. It enables you to resolve emotions left over from work, and prepares you for a relaxing and enjoyable evening. A business executive told me recently that Vivation saved his marriage by helping him handle his anger first, before he brought it home to his wife. Sometimes the practice of having a drink right after work, in an attempt to suppress leftover bad feelings, can backfire and lead to blowups at home. A fifteen-minute Vivation break is far more effective.

Many of the benefits that Vivation provides develop over a period of time as you become more skillful with the process. But from the very beginning you will find that Vivation is an excellent way to reduce your stress anytime, anywhere, within just a few minutes. In comparison to other stress-management techniques, Vivation is more relaxing and refreshing than anything else I've ever seen, and I've spent my life exploring such techniques. I don't know of any other method of stress-management that offers even the *possibility* of deep emotional integration to resolve the stress permanently.

Use Vivation to Solve Personal Problems

You can use Vivation to solve long-standing emotional problems and patterns of unwanted results. With Vivation, you solve your own problems within the privacy of your own being, without obsessing about the past or future. During Vivation you focus on the feelings in your body, which means you bring your full attention to the present moment. By feeling the present moment in detail, you can explore the entire life experience of your energy body. And only within the present moment can you give love to your injured feelings in the way that is effective at healing them forever. During your Vivation session, your Vivation Professional does not give you psychological counseling or make any attempt to produce your results for you. Instead you produce your own results and develop your own clarity and insights.

Although Vivation is not therapy (it is self-applied and is not a treatment for any condition) you can use it to enhance the beneficial effects of therapy. It restores emotional harmony more effectively than any mental method can, because it works directly with the emotions that are both the cause and the result of the problem patterns. Many psychotherapists use Vivation to help their clients make emotional adjustments, let go of the past, and live more in the present.

Use Vivation to eliminate negative conditioning from your mind and emotions. All of us have been substantially influenced by negative conditioning. Television and movies program us to believe that violence solves problems. Advertisers constantly hit us with the message that aging is something shameful, something to be feared, resisted and concealed. For centuries, religions have demanded that we inhibit our sexual energy, threatening eternal damnation to keep us in line. Our politicians contrive complex laws specifying ever increasing punishments unless we comply with their vision of correct conduct. Even our well-meaning parents used rewards and punishments to make us conform. But ultimately we must assume responsibility for our own negativity. Even when we can make a case for someone else initially being to blame for our negativity, we are still responsible if we *stay* negative.

So why do people stay negative? Because of suppression—hiding from their own unpleasant emotions. Changing from a negative outlook to a positive one always requires a conscious choice. Suppression causes negative emotions to build up in the unconscious mind, which in turn causes unconsciously motivated behaviors. Behavior based on suppressed negativity produces undesirable results which stimulate negative emotions all over again. When people have a vivid experience of the unpleasant feelings they create for themselves through their own negativity, they can take that opportunity to cultivate a more positive, loving attitude. But more often they choose to suppress and send the whole process through another cycle.

Vivation directly eliminates negativity at its source. Embracing reality as it is—particularly doing so at the feeling level—frees you from negativity on all levels.

Ultimately, living happily is what matters most. Numerous studies have shown that happy, loving, optimistic people are also healthier and more productive. The immune system itself has been proven to respond strongly to positive thoughts and emotions. Vivation is the most direct way there is to increase positivity. It does this at the feeling level, and thus eliminates the possibility of making you ungrounded or out of touch with reality, which can happen if you only paste "positive thinking" on top of your suppressed emotions.

Use Vivation to Deal Effectively with Grief, Depression or Turmoil

Everyone experiences difficult emotions, or even depression, at one time or another. Vivation helps immediately by generating pleasurable energy within your body. This makes it much easier for you to integrate depression or any other feelings you might be experiencing. Vivation allows you to experience your feelings honestly, without being traumatized by them. Love heals everything.

Obviously I am grateful for many different things Vivation has done for me, personally. Perhaps I am most grateful for how Vivation helped me cope with the death of my father. Vivation helped in two big ways. First, it helped me to resolve difficult feelings I had toward my father, while he was still alive. I had a very close relationship with

Dad the last few years of his life, and I know I would not have had that without Vivation. He died unexpectedly in 1985. This was much more emotional for me than I ever could have imagined. Second, Vivation enabled me to experience all my emotions honestly, and integrate them, so that my memories of my father would not be so painful that I would pull away and try not to think of them. Vivation allowed me to grieve deeply and yet stay connected to my own peaceful center. It helped me to function well when my family needed me, and to be able to write and deliver my father's eulogy. Over the years I have been touched many times by the stories other people have told me about how Vivation helped them in times of grief.

Depression is often a result of submerged, unresolved feelings from the past. Even when these feelings come from childhood (or even from prenatal trauma), Vivation allows them to surface gently and be resolved permanently. For depressed people who are able to take responsibility for their own experience, Vivation is a very effective tool, especially when combined with either psychotherapy or a support group. People with excellent Vivation skills, who regularly have complete sessions, experience rapid integration of feelings that would otherwise be depressing.

I have had many, many people tell me of their success at using Vivation to resolve persistent feelings of guilt. Guilt can be difficult to resolve without Vivation, because the guilt will tell you that you deserve to continue suffering! Vivation bypasses this difficulty. With Vivation, once you learn to integrate feelings, you can integrate guilt exactly the same way as any other emotion.

I knew a Vivation client who spent approximately two years in prison for killing her husband during a physical altercation with him. She first learned Vivation during the time she was waiting for trial, and was able to use Vivation during her trial and incarceration. I saw her again several times after she was released, and she said Vivation was extremely helpful in keeping her composure during the trial, and resolving her guilt, fear, and loneliness while she was in prison. She said it helped enormously in returning to a normal life after she was released.

Vivation is extremely valuable during times of personal turmoil because it allows you to deal with your feelings honestly without having the emotions muddle your mind. Vivation connects you with the energy of renewal within you and gives you the strength and courage to carry on. Vivation can be called a feeling-level prayer. It gives mental clarity and spiritual direction in the midst of emotional turbulence.

Vivation also makes you more emotionally available to others. People are commonly unable to be sensitive to the emotional needs of others because their own emotional needs are not being met. As you integrate your own feelings, you will naturally provide a beacon of hope to others and help them move toward integration as well.

Vivation reliably connects you with your inner resourcefulness. It increases your motivation and improves your concentration, even during the most difficult of times.

Use Vivation To Improve Your Breathing

Most people are not very good breathers. Circular Breathing not only harmonizes the energy in your body immediately, but is also the best way to breathe all the time. Circular Breathing is relaxed and does not produce hyperventilation. What it does do is open the energy channels of your body. The bliss you feel during Vivation is a result of your spiritual energy flowing freely. Suppression of emotions requires inhibition of breathing. Every time you integrate a feeling, your breathing improves automatically.

Circular Breathing does not produce hyperventilation and does not get you "high on oxygen." The marvelous, blissful feelings you experience through Vivation come from resolving suppressed emotions and restoring your connection with your spiritual essence. Vivation makes you feel good in the same way that prayer, meditation and forgiveness make you feel good, but very physically.

Breathing exercises that give no focus to integrating emotions are very limited in their ability to make permanent improvements to the breathing you do normally. This is because suppression of emotions requires an inhibition of your breathing. Integration of suppressed emotions makes it possible to breathe more freely, because after integration, you have no covert payoff in continuing to inhibit your breathing.

A few years ago I had a client who is an extremely successful designer of computer software. All his life he was severely asthmatic. After just a few Vivation sessions with me he was able to give up his medications and inhalers for the first time in his memory. I have seen Vivation produce similar results many, many times.

I have a friend who has suffered his whole life from chronic apnea, which affects him both when he's asleep and when he's awake. Vivation has not completely cured his apnea, but he says that during the day he can feel apnea consciously and take a full breath. He says it has dramatically improved his life.

Vivation improves your breathing in at least three important ways:

1. It gives you training and concentrated practice in proper breathing.
2. Each integration clears the energy pathways in order to make breathing more efficient.
3. Integration of emotions makes you *want* to breathe more fully throughout your life.

People with various kinds of breathing difficulties usually notice immediate and lasting improvement in their breathing as a result of Vivation. People who already have excellent breathing also notice improvements as a result of Vivation.

Use Vivation To Improve Your Relationships

People have trouble in relationships when they don't accept each other as they are. Unresolved emotions from childhood and later stages of life can often be projected onto other people. Vivation eliminates old patterns of negativity and makes it possible to see people (including oneself) as the magnificent beings they really are. Vivation will make you more loving while at the same time helping you to acknowledge problems with people while the problems are still subtle. As a result, all your relationships with everyone improve dramatically.

I know a man who used to work as the pastor at a church in San Francisco with a substantially gay congregation. There came a time when everyone in the congregation either had HIV or knew someone with AIDS. His work changed. Previously his main work had been helping people come back to the Church when they felt that the Church had abandoned them. But then his main work became helping people renew their spirituality in the face of terror and bereavement. He not only kept his own spirits up by Viving, he also introduced many parishioners to the process and said it was the most valuable tool he had ever found for helping people make a personal connection with the Holy Spirit.

My observation is that most people relate to God and their parents in about the same way. They obsess about the judgments that God and their parents make about them, and they miss the real source of stress in their relationships with their parents and with God: that they judge God and their parents negatively.

If you find fault with how your parents raised you, then you carry with you the belief that you are damaged. This results in reduced self-esteem and many other problems. Vivation makes it possible to accept your parents as they are, and only this makes it possible to accept yourself as you are.

Whenever you make anything wrong, you judge God negatively. Only by accepting reality fully, can you make peace with God. Thus every integration improves your relationship with God.

Romantic relationships improve dramatically as a result of Vivation. Every negative judgment that you have about yourself or about your partner restricts the flow of loving energy between you. Integrating these feelings makes your relationship deeper, more loving, freer, and more spontaneous.

Use Vivation To Develop Your Spirituality

Vivation enables you to experience the divine directly, without religion or belief systems. Nowadays, many people want to be spiritual without having to be religious. Vivation allows you to do just that. Vivation increases your spiritual autonomy. Many people, unfortunately, try to substitute mental concepts or "theology" for direct spiritual experience. Such belief systems are toxic in their effect because people substitute them for the real thing. Mental substitutes for real spiritual experience erect an even thicker barrier between consciousness and spirit, and leave people open to manipulation by cult leaders and religious authority figures. Vivation directly counteracts the negative effects of toxic belief systems by providing genuine spiritual experience within the privacy of one's own being.

Vivation increases contact between your consciousness and your spirit. Your spirit is very different from your mind. Many people are so completely cut off from experiencing their own spirit that they even think that they *are* their mind! Even the first Vivation session increases contact between your consciousness and your individual spirit. Over many sessions your contact becomes continuous and your knowledge of yourself becomes far deeper. Eventually, your identity changes and you experience yourself as a spirit utilizing a mind, rather than a mind with a vague sense of spirit.

I know a woman who has practiced meditation for more than twenty years. She says that in the past she would get to a very peaceful place through meditation, but it was always a detached place, somehow "outside herself." Now with Vivation, she says she gets to a more blissful state than ever, finding the oneness of all things within the emotional energy in her body.

Everyone needs spiritual renewal. Daily life presents so many challenges and puts us in contact with so many annoying people, that we all need periodic renewal just to keep from plunging into despair. It is no coincidence that the word inspiration means both "breathing in" and "the energy, ideals and reverence of the spirit." Your own individual spirit never despairs, because it knows the long-term picture of your evolution. Vivation gives you a visceral, palpable connection to your spirit, using your breath to draw your spirit into your body and mind. When you experience the Eternal Divine *within* the arduous mundane, integration pulls you out of the quagmire, back into the celestial realms.

Vivation also increases your inspiration and enthusiasm when you're already feeling well. Every contact with your own individual spirit raises your energy to a higher frequency. Every integration of a negative emotion makes you mindful of the miraculous nature of your life. I know Buddhist monks and traditional Hindus who use Vivation as one of their primary spiritual practices. They say they find Vivation to be an extremely valuable adjunct to their more traditional meditations and devotional services, exactly because it allows them to remain grounded while experiencing the spiritual states they seek. Every benefit that Vivation conveys really comes from this process of making the divine more manifest in your experience of ordinary life.

Vivation also develops the spiritual courage necessary to take action on decisions. My definition of courage is "moving ahead with purposeful action even though you know that doing so will activate strong emotions." Vivation increases your knowledge of what you truly desire, and gives you the sense that you can handle the emotions that come from anything that happens. As each integration reduces emotional resistance to action and change, it simultaneously develops a greater sense of purpose.

Courage is an essential ingredient in living well. Most people think that some people simply are courageous and other people simply not, as though they were born that way. Vivation reliably makes both courageous people and less courageous people more courageous. At the same time,

Vivation also makes people less fool-hardy. This is because Vivation keeps you constantly in touch with all parts of yourself, wise and foolish, suppressive and integrative. Vivation continuously increases your conscious contact with the sage counsel of your innermost discernment.

Vivation is profoundly spiritual. It works by connecting your consciousness with your own individual spirit. God can only be found in the present moment. In fact, nothing exists other than God. If you're not experiencing God right now, it is because of suppression. Vivation directly counteracts that suppression and provides a direct experience of God within your own body—the most satisfying experience there is.

Vivation provides you with clarity. This is because your feeling awareness is more connected to your spirit than your thinking mind is. Your spirit reliably knows what's best for you. Emotions always come into play in decision-making, no matter how logical you believe yourself to be. Vivation resolves your emotions and enables you to feel the will of your spirit.

Vivation is unparalleled in its ability to develop mental clarity. The only reason why we ever have trouble knowing what course of action is best for us is because of suppression. Our spirit always knows what's best for us. A Vivation session, taken through to its natural point of completion, always gives clarity. A benefit of continuing use of Vivation is that your wisdom in making decisions will increase dramatically as your conscious contact with your own individual spirit increases.

Over the years I have seen literally hundreds of people use Vivation to make the transition from working at jobs to being successfully self-employed. Self-employment is not for everyone, but many people find that they can increase their income and their fulfillment simultaneously by becoming self-employed doing work they love. Vivation integrates fear and other emotions that are activated during the transition, and gives you the spiritual courage and resourcefulness you need to be successful.

Sometimes Vivation helps a person make a wise decision *not* to do something. I know a man who owns a small company. Several years ago a key employee began making a lot of mistakes, missing deadlines, and showing up late for work. Repeated attempts at correction failed, and after one particularly costly mistake, the man felt a strong impulse to fire his employee, but he hesitated, and took the time to give himself a Vivation session. He decided not to fire the employee but to have a heart-to-heart talk with him instead, at which time he learned that his employee's long-time best friend was dying of cancer. The employee was so grateful that his boss had not fired him, and had taken the time to show his concern, that he soon became more effective in his work than ever before, and served the company well for several more years.

Use Vivation To Feel Better Fast

Whenever you're feeling bad, for any emotional or physical reason, you can use Vivation to feel better fast. Vivation empowers you to make peace with everything you feel. Integrating a feeling causes appropriate change to take place in your mind, body and energy. You can integrate anger, fatigue, headache, body aches, and agitation. While complete resolution of any of these conditions might require a full session, even the first few minutes of Vivation make you feel significantly better. Just as important, Vivation improves your perspective about what has been bothering you.

Everyone has physical pain from time to time. Some people have chronic physical pain that troubles them every day of their lives. Vivation is an effective method for coping with physical pain, whether acute or chronic. The subjective experience of suffering with physical pain is a result of an ill relationship between consciousness and experience. This is exactly what Vivation works on. Vivation permits the integration of physical pain.

Many people who previously suffered with chronic headaches say that Vivation not only gives relief once the headache is under way, but also stops their headaches from developing if they use it right away when they feel a headache starting.

Vivation works very effectively to help women going through childbirth. The breathing in Vivation is not used as a distraction from the pain of labor but instead helps the mother integrate the physical pain and to be more consciously present with the miracle of birth. Many women who have given birth both before and after learning Vivation say that they are amazed at the difference Vivation made for themselves and their babies.

An infinitely different kind of pain is experienced the day after an evening of drinking too much. Vivation is an effective way to integrate hangovers! The malaise, lethargy and headache all respond well to Vivation. Regular use of Vivation may also decrease the desire for alcohol.

I know a woman who was in a horrible car accident and nearly killed. She needed months of rehabilitation after suffering numerous burns and broken bones. She says that because she used Vivation her pain, although severe, was much more bearable than anyone expected. She also says that with Vivation she was able to integrate emotions that would otherwise have, themselves, been debilitating.

Every now and then I have a day when, for no apparent reason, I just don't feel good physically. When that happens, I might feel tired, stiff and vaguely sick. Sometimes when that happens I have weird impulses for things to do about it, from unusual food cravings to wanting caffeine or alcohol. When instead I take a Vivation break I always find that within a few minutes the bad feeling is gone, and I feel well and happy again. And it's all natural!

Use Vivation To Break Bad Habits And Addictions

Bad habits and compulsive patterns of behavior exist for the purpose of suppressing emotions. Integrating the suppressed feelings eliminates the perceived need to engage in the suppressive behavior. Often, bad habits drop away spontaneously as a result of Vivation. With particularly troublesome habitual behaviors, make Vivation a key part of your program of behavior modification.

Vivation has been shown to be effective in helping people in recovery from addictions. It works well in conjunction with Twelve-Step Programs, such as Alcoholics Anonymous. Vivation helps in recovery by freeing people from the past, increasing motivation through enthusiasm, and developing emotional resourcefulness to find new solutions to old problems. It also shows you how to feel incredibly good without resorting to the addictive behavior.

Ceasing to engage in a habitual behavior sometimes produces unpleasant emotions and physical sensations. Vivation makes it possible to integrate these sensations into your sense of well-being and eliminate the discomfort. I have known hundreds of people who have used Vivation to quit smoking. Vivation makes the emotions and physical effects of nicotine withdrawal downright comfortable.

A friend of mine habitually drove much faster than the speed limit. Almost every time he got on the freeway he would drive a hundred miles an hour or more—a felony in California. He knew this was dangerous and that he needed to stop, but felt a compulsion to speed that was born of rebelliousness. No government was going to tell him how to drive! He had a Vivation session with me in which he obviously went deeply within himself. He told me afterward that at no time during the session did he think about driving, but he realized on his way home from the session that he felt different. He said his compulsion to speed had left him. He has been a safe driver (and less compulsively rebellious in other ways, too) ever since.

Use Vivation To Cause Creative Breakthrough

Vivation increases your creativity by reducing the barrier between your subconscious creative process (from which your dreams originate) and your conscious will. It focuses your creativity on solving your problems appropriately. All creative breakthrough comes about through shifting your attention from what isn't there to what is. That is exactly what integration is! Every integration you achieve through Vivation gives you a creative breakthrough. Most important, with Vivation you cause creative breakthrough at the feeling level, thus bypassing the mental inflexibility that made it difficult to solve the problem in the first place.

Creativity is not only for the arts. Enhanced creativity has enormous practical value for anyone. You can use your creativity to be more effective in business, in relationships, in your health—in any situation where you are responsible for producing results.

I know an attorney who uses Vivation all the time in his work. He says that before he learned Vivation he often felt unsure how to proceed, but now he is able to come up with a creative strategy by just Viving into his feelings for a few minutes.

Use Vivation To Achieve Your Goals

Fulfilling your heart-felt desires is the most natural thing in the world. Unfortunately, people create unnecessary difficulties for themselves by suppressing their emotions. The suppression itself consumes time and energy, and then the suppressed emotion creates problems by influencing behavior inappropriately from the unconscious level. Vivation makes your goals clearer to you, because in the integrated state you feel the guidance of your spirit. It clears the emotional blockage that can create struggle and self-sabotage. Vivation makes it easy to take appropriate action with enthusiasm.

Countless salespeople have used Vivation to increase their sales by becoming more comfortable communicating with customers. Musicians, performers, athletes and public speakers find Vivation invaluable as a way to develop comfort, relaxation, and poise.

Vivation is extremely useful during the planning stages of any project. By including your feelings, Vivation makes it possible to "think with more of yourself." Often a plan will mentally seem fine, but by exploring the subtle emotional responses to it, potential difficulties with troubled feelings will be highlighted. Integration of the feelings results in creative breakthroughs that solve the problems—problems that otherwise would not have come to light until the plan was put into action, when it is too late!

Many times an obstacle to implementing a plan is not an intrinsic difficulty, but only a perceived difficulty, or an emotional resistance to taking necessary action. Vivation resolves the emotion and makes it possible to proceed with clarity and self-confidence.

Use Vivation To Raise Your Self-Esteem

You have self-esteem to the extent that you love yourself unconditionally. Shame and guilt rob you of self-esteem. Vivation resolves shame and guilt gently, thoroughly and permanently. No matter where the shame or guilt came from in the first place, when you give unconditional love to your troubled feelings they heal themselves spontaneously. Through Vivation you find peace of mind.

If you want to know yourself better, Vivation is the ultimate. Vivation is a flawless mirror. Ordinary optical mirrors use light to reveal your external features. Vivation is a feeling-level mirror that uses your own life-energy to reveal every secret of your body, mind, and spirit. The importance of this is illustrated by the principle: *If you don't love yourself infinitely, it's because you haven't gotten to know yourself well enough yet.*

For most people, trying to learn about themselves by simply feeling their bodies is like trying to see themselves in a mirror while sitting in a dark room. No matter how good the mirror, you need to turn on the light. Vivation uses Circular Breathing to illuminate your feeling awareness of your body. Circular Breathing does not change the way you feel, any more than turning on the light changes the way you look. It simply enables you to experience the detail within the feelings already present in your body.

Sometimes, when people are burdened by too much responsibility for too long of a time, they realize that they really don't know themselves. I remember a client of mine who, in her early fifties, had the last of her children move out, and almost immediately was divorced by her husband. After she used Vivation to resolve the feelings of loss and separation, it dawned on her that she had never before had the opportunity to find out who she really was! She discovered, with the help of Vivation, that she had a great talent for writing. She enrolled in creative writing classes at the university, had some stories published, and last I knew was working on a novel.

An unfortunate effect of suppression is that it not only deletes your awareness of the feelings you wish to avoid, it also cuts off the helpful awareness of yourself that you *could* have by feeling the emotion. Only through gaining deep knowledge of yourself can you truly heal yourself. Every Vivation session is an amazing adventure into your inner world, an exploration that must produce healing simply through learning the truth.

Use Vivation To Live Your Life To Its Fullest

Vivation enhances your enjoyment of everything. It makes both pleasant and unpleasant experiences better. There is always pleasurable energy in your body as long as you are alive. Vivation enhances the flow of this energy and allows you to find pleasure where you wouldn't find it otherwise.

Vivation is a meditation on how wonderful the present moment is. It is a meditation on the feelings in the body, in which you invite the worst of your feelings to come up, but integrate them into your sense of well-being.

Vivation enhances your enjoyment of everything you do. It makes both pleasurable activities (such as making love) and unpleasant activities (such as paying taxes) more pleasurable.

Vivation makes any pleasurable activity more pleasurable by bringing you into the present moment, where the pleasure actually exists. It resolves emotions that can limit your pleasure, such as fear, guilt and shame. It also increases your receptivity to the good available in the moment. Vivation allows you to let go of being distracted by your own mind. For this reason, Vivation greatly enhances the pleasure of attending a concert, eating a dessert, or receiving a massage.

Vivation enhances your sense of humor. It does this both by increasing your mental flexibility, so you can see things from a different point of view, and by making you more receptive to positive experiences. In terms of its physiological effects, Vivation is related to laughter. When you experience your spirit dancing within you, of course you do not take life too seriously!

Vivation makes you happier in many different ways. The main thing that limits people's happiness is unresolved emotions, and you resolve these emotions with Vivation. Vivation unblocks the energy channels that allow joy and love to flow freely. Vivation helps you make positive changes in your life, put an end to bad situations, and become more effective at achieving your goals.

The one benefit that more people have reported to me than any other is increased happiness and well-being. Literally thousands of people have expressed to me their gratitude for the way Vivation has improved their relationships, their family lives, and their general satisfaction with life.

Just last week, a client said to me, "Since my last session with you I haven't stopped smiling! I feel good all the time. Everyone is telling me that I seem like a different person and they keep asking me what happened!"

You can use Vivation to be more present, aware and grounded throughout your life. The skills you learn in Vivation are the very essence of "being here now". Most people, most of the time, are preoccupied with the past or future. They worry about the future. They long for the past or wish that the past had been different somehow. Only by being fully present can you experience joy. And only by being present can you be alert to opportunities (or dangers) as they present themselves.

Once you have gained some mastery over Vivation, you will be able to use it anytime, anyplace, even while engaging in other activities. You can use it while driving, talking on the telephone, asking your boss for a raise, making love, feeling emotions about the day, or when you're trying to fall asleep at night. Vivation in Action allows you to resolve emotions immediately when they come up.

As you progress through a series of sessions with your Vivation Professional, he or she might lead you through some "Vivation-in-Action Adventures." These are Vivation sessions in which you Vive while doing something else, in order to integrate the feelings produced by the activity. There are infinite possibilities for Vivation-in-

Action Adventures. Here are a few: Viving in warm or cold water, Viving in church, Viving on a roller coaster, Viving while striking up a conversation at a singles bar.

Many professional athletes have learned to use Vivation. Not only does Vivation increase their endurance and other aspects of their performance, it also reduces their injuries by making them more present in what they are doing.

In situations such as giving a public presentation or any kind of performance, Vivation is invaluable. It enables you to resolve your fear and performance anxiety, to use your emotional energy to your benefit, to be fully present with your audience, to be in contact with every part of yourself, and to be your absolute best.

Vivation shifts your awareness to the positive aspect of your experience. It directly increases the flow of love-energy in your body and raises your self-esteem. This makes you realize that you deserve the good things in life. Combined with the way Vivation solves your problems and increases your creativity and enthusiasm for achieving goals, Vivation enables you to live a far richer life than you ever dreamed possible.

CHAPTER 2

HOW VIVATION WORKS

Happiness is a skill. As with other skills, you can get better at it. There are two separate skills involved in living well. One is the skill of achieving your goals. The other skill is something most people never think of as being a skill: the skill of enjoying what you already have. Although getting what you want is obviously important, the skill of being happy right now is even more important. You'll be more successful at achieving your goals if you know how to be happy every step along the way. You won't dissipate energy on friction. You'll be alert to unexpected opportunities. And you'll generate enthusiasm continuously, which will move you joyfully toward your ultimate fulfillment.

Vivation enables you to be happy with what you've already got. First of all, "what you've got" is the present moment. That's all you've got and that's everything there is. That you exist to be experiencing anything at all is vastly more significant than any particular thing you might experience.

Within every human is the remembrance that existence, itself, is fundamentally miraculous. Beyond the stream of activity and worries is a centered space of wisdom and perfection. The more we remain consciously connected with this perfection-consciousness, the more quickly, and less stressful, we gain the satisfaction that comes from living well.

In spite of this, most people think they can feel happy only under special circumstances, when everything is going their way. They expend their energy wishing things were different, struggling to make things different, or trying to escape from their feelings about things being the way they are. What a lot of needless suffering!

Your degree of happiness is determined by your *attitude* about what happens in your life, not by the things, themselves, that happen. Every adversity contains the seed of an equal or greater opportunity. Finding the good buried within the unpleasant is an art.

I have known many people with severe physical disabilities who were happier than most able-bodied people. I'll never forget the time a college friend of mine, paralyzed from the neck down, told me that because of what he'd learned about life from being quadriplegic, he was grateful he'd had his accident!

What he had learned is that *existence itself is infinitely valuable*.

Consider a man who believes that what would make him happy is to own a Mercedes. No matter how strong his belief, he is wrong; he can be happy owning no car at all—if he decides to be. The truth is, *only he can make himself happy*.

The only thing absolutely necessary for your happiness is your own existence. But you only experience happiness to the degree that you allow yourself to receive, in the depth of your being, the good available in the present moment, with everything exactly the way it is. Again, this is a skill and you can get better at it.

That people find so much to complain about is not a sign of how bad their lives are, but a sign of how poor their skill of happiness is.

What does it take to enjoy every moment unconditionally? What is this skill of happiness?

Simply put, it is the skill of not making yourself unhappy. You don't have to do anything special to enjoy something. Because your existence is miraculous, enjoyment is natural and available in every moment.

In order to *not* enjoy something, you must block your awareness of what is good about it, and block your awareness that existence itself is fundamentally good. People do this by insisting that what they are experiencing *should* be different from how it is. Doing so separates them from the reality of their situation and shifts their attention from the good in what they're experiencing to the gap between how it is and how they think it should be. The term I use for this is "make-wrong."

You make something wrong when you compare it to an imaginary standard, such as "how it should be," "how you wish it were," "what somebody else has," "how good things used to be back in the good old days," and so on.

I'm sure you've noticed, by this point in your life, that things are not the way you think they should be. Things are the way they are. Your ability to be happy depends on your ability to be in harmony with reality *as it is*.

This does not mean you give up making things better—quite the opposite. But consider this: Even if you succeed at making things better five minutes from now, that does you no good *right now*. Only your ability to improve your relationship to things as they are right now can make you happier.

You Contexts Define Your Reality

Your relationship to what you are experiencing is called the "context" in which you hold the experience. Whenever you experience anything, you hold it in one particular context, just as whenever you look at something, you see it from one particular perspective. You can change contexts quickly, but you can only use one context at a time. It is impossible to think about anything without having a context. You can either choose your context consciously, or you can let your subconscious mind choose your context for you, which often means contaminating fresh, new situations with stale, old negativity.

The way something affects you is determined by the context in which you hold it. You can hold anything in a context that makes you inspired and creative, or you can hold the same thing in a context that makes you helpless and depressed. You always have the choice.

Negativity can be defined as contexts that reduce your happiness. A negative context is any context in which you compare something to an imaginary standard and decide that what you are imagining would be better than reality.

To clarify this point, you only make something wrong, and cause yourself problems, by telling yourself that what you're experiencing should be different *right now* from how it is. Suppose you are building a house and are looking at a vacant lot with piles of lumber and building materials. There is no limit to how happy you can be—as long as it's OK with you that the house is in your future, and wood, nails, and plans for hard work are in your present. But if you tell yourself, "It's July and the job should be done by now," then you are separating yourself from reality and needlessly reducing your happiness.

A *positive context* is any context in which you embrace reality as it is, without comparing it to an imaginary standard. A positive context not only makes you happier than a negative context, it also makes you more effective. When you hold your current situation in a positive context, you focus on what's useful, instead of complaining about how bad things are.

Additionally, a positive context increases your motivation, since it enables you to be motivated by enthusiasm. People often expect negativity to be a good source of motivation, but it is not. If negativity really motivated people, then the most negative people would be the most productive. What actually happens is that the most negative people commit suicide and produce nothing. Cultivating enthusiasm increases motivation and productivity.

Every shift from focusing on what-isn't-there-that-should-be-there to focusing on what-is-there-that's-useful, produces a creative breakthrough, a quantum leap in effectiveness.

Once people have decided that something is "bad" or lacking in some way, they often have difficulty changing to a positive context, for a variety of reasons having to do with suppression. Vivation easily eliminates these difficulties, and is the simplest, quickest, most reliable method for eliminating negativity that there is.

Vivation works at the feeling level and thus bypasses the traps of mental processing. Just as you have a variety of senses through which you perceive the world around you, you have parallel "senses" through which you perceive your thoughts and memories, your inner world. Everybody is to some extent internally visual, internally verbal, and internally feeling. All these internal senses are interconnected and operate continuously, whether or not you are aware of them. Let's explore the feeling sense, since it is important in Vivation.

You have feelings about everything. Whenever you give your attention to a particular thing, be it "external" or "internal," you feel something about it. The feeling you get is specific. You get a different feeling for each different thing you think about. For example, when you think about different people, you get a different feeling about each one. And you get a different feeling when you think about a lawnmower than when you think about a plate of spaghetti.

Whenever you make anything wrong, you simultaneously make your corresponding feeling wrong. This means that whenever you find fault with something, you get an unpleasant feeling in your body. However, when you stop making that thing wrong, your corresponding feeling not only stops feeling uncomfortable, it becomes a source of pleasure.

Here's the most important idea in this whole chapter: *By changing your relationship to your feeling about something, you change your relationship to the thing itself.*

Vivation gives you the ability to feel your feelings, experience them vividly, and *enjoy* them!

Enjoying an "unpleasant" feeling is much easier than it sounds. People talk about their "negative" emotions as though they don't enjoy them, but they act as though they do enjoy them. For example, most people would say they don't like feeling afraid, yet scary movies do billions of dollars of business every year! If people didn't enjoy sadness they wouldn't listen to sad songs. If they didn't like feeling angry they wouldn't watch the news. Words like "sadness" and "fear" are only labels, anyway, applied by the mind to a physical experience. The feeling of *aliveness* in the body is always pleasurable, even when the aliveness takes the form of an emotion—provided you don't resist feeling the emotion. By feeling your emotions honestly, while enjoying your aliveness unconditionally, you produce tremendous benefits for yourself.

Integration

Emotions are like everything else: when you don't make them wrong they contribute to your benefit and pleasure. Ceasing to make an emotion wrong causes the feeling to *integrate* into your sense of well-being. All the unpleasantness spontaneously disappears and you gain a fresh and positive perspective on whatever the feeling was about. Because Vivation causes something that had seemed bad to integrate into your sense of well-being, we call the result of Vivation "integration." Integration means giving your attention to what you have been making wrong and receiving all of the good it has for you.

I'll explain integration with an analogy. Someone asked a great yogi, "What should we eat?" His reply: "The question is not what should you eat, but what can you digest!" Integration means digesting your life experiences. Anytime you experience upset, it's because you haven't digested some experience. The experience will continue to upset you until you finally do digest it. The reason you haven't digested it before now is because you've developed a habit of suppressing the feeling whenever it comes up, putting it off until another day.

In Vivation your body gently presents the feeling you most need to digest. Then you relax and surrender, allowing your body to digest the experience. When you integrate an experience, you receive what's useful in it and completely let go of what isn't useful.

You can integrate anything in your life that has been bothering you, and you have a choice about how you do it. You can integrate something mentally by choosing a positive context for it. Or, you can integrate it physically by embracing the feeling it produces in your body.

Integrating at the feeling level is better in many ways. Feeling is immediate and thinking is not. You can feel and integrate your emotions about something instantaneously, whereas using your mind to try and figure out what's good about it might take a very long time. A benefit of working at the feeling level is that feelings are inherently honest. Mentally, you can confuse yourself for years at a time, but your honest feelings stay with you. Another benefit of processing at the feeling level is that you can feel the integration happen. Mental processes often leave a lingering doubt about whether you have done enough to achieve a lasting result. In Vivation, you focus right on the feeling that has been troubling you and you *feel* the exact moment it integrates.

Finally, a tremendous benefit of working at the feeling level is that you can use breathing to enhance your ability to integrate your feelings.

Vivation utilizes a specific breathing skill to connect you consciously with the good that is present in all your feelings. The breathing itself does not cause the result; integration is caused by exploring and embracing the feeling. The breathing skill helps enormously by developing an energy-level rapport with the feeling. Learning to harmonize your breathing with each feeling as it comes up makes exploring the feeling—and enjoying it—much easier.

If you don't know how to integrate your feelings, you suppress the feelings you find unpleasant. Suppression does not make your feelings go away. Instead, your suppressed feelings remain active in your mind and body, causing behavior and situations that recreate the very emotions from which you tried to escape. Vivation enables you to *gently and voluntarily* reexperience your suppressed feelings and integrate them.

When a "negative" feeling is explored in detail and loved in totality, it transforms—the energy remains but the negativity disappears. The transformations go something like this: anger, when loved, turns into determination; sadness, explored and enjoyed, becomes gratitude; fear, when felt in detail and embraced as positive energy, turns out to be alertness. When all feelings are allowed and appreciated, the experience of their energy is the experience of unconditional love. You cannot love unconditionally as long as there are any emotions that you do not enjoy. Trying to love on the condition that no one does anything to activate unwanted emotions is not love at all, but a kind of bargaining.

This healing process does not come about by *trying* to feel gratitude when sadness comes up, or *trying* to experience determination when you feel anger. It means allowing the sadness and anger—totally.

To allow yourself to experience your emotions does not mean you act them out by raging or dumping on people. Emotional healing does not come about through expressing every emotion, although appropriate expression of emotion—sharing yourself as you are—is essential for healthy relationships. All emotional healing comes about by embracing reality. Every decision to make something wrong—to insist that something should be other than the way it actually is—withdraws you from reality. Vivation allows you to embrace feelings at a deeper level within yourself. By embracing your feeling about something, exactly as they are, you bring yourself one step closer to total awareness and total love.

I also want to emphasize that Vivation is not only for emotions. Emotions are an important part of life, and they illustrate how integration works, but Vivation also works on energy that cannot really be called emotion (fatigue for example) and on physical pain. Vivation really works on anything you can feel, which, given Vivation's ability to eliminate suppression, really means absolutely everything.

The skill of Vivation has Five Elements:

1. **Circular Breathing**
2. **Complete Relaxation**
3. **Awareness in Detail**
4. **Integration into Ecstasy**
5. **Do Whatever You Do—Willingness is Enough**

Each one of The Five Elements is a skill in its own right, and each represents a body of knowledge.

Vivation is not five separate processes, but is one process which is best described in terms of five component skills. During a Vivation session you do all Five Elements simultaneously. Your skill with The Five Elements enables you to produce results in your Vivation sessions. I'll explain each of The Five Elements in detail in the following chapters of this book, and I'll explain how you can easily stay in all Five Elements by focusing your attention on doing only one thing at a time.

Vivation Professionals

The people who teach The Five Elements of Vivation are called Vivation Professionals. There are Vivation Professionals throughout the world. Every Vivation Professional has the goal of teaching you to use Vivation by yourself in your day-to-day life.

When you go to a Vivation Professional you receive profound healing, but even more important than that, you also learn to cause the results for yourself. Each Vivation session is as much a learning experience as a healing experience. You, the *Viver*, produce all the results in your session. No one can do it for you. Only you can allow your suppressed material to come up and only you can focus your awareness on it. Only you can make the decision to stop making your feelings wrong and embrace them.

In your first Vivation session, your Vivation Professional will lead you through some experiential exercises to teach you the Five Elements. Then, with his or her support and guidance, you will *Vive*, giving yourself a fascinating and deeply pleasurable experience. At first you'll Vive lying down or sitting. After a few sessions, you'll learn to Vive while engaging in other activities.

From then on you can use Vivation anytime, anywhere to cause emotional resolution, creative breakthrough, and heightened enjoyment of whatever you're experiencing.

CHAPTER 3

THE FIVE ELEMENTS OF VIVATION

Vivation directly expands love. The results of Vivation come from allowing your body to present you with your feelings about people, things, and situations that you do not presently love, and then giving your love to those feelings. Every integration is a quantum leap in your awareness and your receptivity to goodness. Every integration is a decision to love. Every make-wrong is a decision not to love. Every decision not to love someone or something reduces your happiness, your aliveness, your awareness, and your effectiveness. Every make-wrong, every decision not to love, causes problems for you. The more stubbornly you cling to your negativity, the more problems your negativity produces for you. Vivation exists to free you from the toxic effects of your negativity and to give you the benefits that come from manifesting your loving spirit into your life.

Whenever you don't love something, your mind will say to you that it's because that thing is not lovable. This is never true, however. Your own refusal to love is always the only obstacle. Because you are responsible for the decision not to love, you are also responsible for changing your mind and deciding to love.

Vivation is not a treatment, applied from the outside, to help with any condition. Only you can produce the results of Vivation for yourself. When you go to a Vivation Professional, he or she will teach you the internal skill of Viving, and will guide you through your sessions. But you have to take complete responsibility for your own results. One hundred percent of your healing is produced from the inside by you.

How do you produce healing within yourself? Through application of The Five Elements of Vivation.

The Component Skills of Vivation

I developed The Five Elements in 1979 as the culmination of more than a decade's research into what was effective in personal development. Since then I have spent virtually all my time refining my own use of The Five Elements and my ability to teach them to others.

The Five Elements of Vivation are skills. Even before you ever learn anything about The Five Elements, you already possess some degree of skill with each of them. As you learn about Vivation and give yourself Vivation sessions, you will continue to gain mastery over The Five Elements. Living The Five Elements totally in every moment is exactly the same thing as *enlightenment*.

The Five Elements are not steps, applied sequentially; they are components of one single skill, the skill of Vivation. All Five Elements need to be present simultaneously in order to achieve integration. And when all five are present, integration happens automatically!

Each of The Five Elements comprises a substantial body of knowledge. You can get started with Vivation, and have an extremely satisfying healing experience, with only a very limited knowledge of The Five Elements. But your experience in your first session will lead you to want to master the process. To master Vivation you must develop thorough knowledge of The Five Elements—not just an intellectual understanding of them, but a real working knowledge of how to use them during your sessions.

This does not mean that you need to keep a lot of knowledge running through your mind during your sessions. Once you have knowledge of The Five Elements you can easily stay in all Five Elements by focusing your attention on doing just one thing with your full attention. Chapter 9 of this book explains that thoroughly.

As you go through a series of Vivation sessions, you get a sense of which of The Five Elements you are most skillful with, and which one you most need to cultivate further. Sometimes you can use your strongest Element to help you cultivate the one you most need to develop. Your Vivation Professional will help you become more skillful with each of The Five Elements, especially with the one Element that needs the most help.

The same Five Elements integrate everything. To cause integration you need only feel your feelings honestly and thoroughly and to relate to them in a positive way. The exact same skills integrate guilt as integrate shyness. The same skills integrate a headache as enhance the pleasure of walking in nature. You can apply The Five Elements equally well to grief about leaving a relationship as to apprehension about starting a new job. The skills of The Five Elements are universal.

The Five Elements are all there is to Vivation. You don't need to supplement them with anything else. You don't need bodywork. You don't need affirmations. You don't need psychotherapy. You don't need drugs. You don't need talking about your problems. You don't need accompanying music. The Five Elements, all by themselves, make it possible to integrate anything, no matter what it is. All these other things may have their place in a happy life, but they are not part of Vivation. Any difficulty anybody ever has with Vivation is solved by improving their skill with one or more of The Five Elements.

Vivation never needs to be intense. During sessions, feelings generally start off subtle and gradually become more intense. Even when the feelings were intense at the time you suppressed them, you have the opportunity to integrate them when they first arise and are still very subtle. You can always integrate your feelings when they are subtle, simply by paying attention to them. In Chapter 4, I explain how to adjust your breathing during your session in order to make your session either more intense or less intense as you wish. One of the great benefits of Vivation is that it allows you to easily integrate emotions in your sessions, so they never have to explode uncontrollably in your life.

The Safety of Vivation

Vivation is perfectly safe. Vivation cannot bring up any feelings that you don't already have. You are safer being aware of feelings than not being aware of them. If you are not conscious of your feelings, then they influence your behavior from the unconscious level, and produce results you do not consciously want. When you are conscious of your feelings, you have a choice about what to do, and your feelings actually help you take appropriate action. Furthermore, when your feelings are suppressed, you have the illusion that they would be overwhelming if they came out of suppression. With Vivation, you manage all your feelings quite well, and are never overwhelmed by them. Since you learn how to adjust the level of intensity of your session before you ever begin, Vivation has no more chance of being too intense for you than does a self-massage. In fact, you are safer doing Vivation than not doing Vivation.

The Five Elements cannot be understood by their names alone. They need to be taught with experiential exercises under the guidance of someone who uses them regularly. Knowledge *about* The Five Elements can come from listening or reading, but knowledge *of how to use them* can come only from receiving sessions from a Vivation Professional. At the back of this book is a list of Vivation Professionals and a toll-free number you can call to get a more up-to-date list.

The Five Elements give you the ability to "be here now." *Being here now* means full awareness of the present moment, including the aspects of the present moment that have heretofore remained hidden. Much of what is hidden in the unconscious mind is suppressed because of the expectation that it would be unpleasant if it were experienced consciously. Vivation makes it easy to find pleasure in these feelings, and because of that Vivation makes it easy to have access to them. Besides allowing suppressed feelings to surface, being here now also means being attentive to the ever-changing subtle energies of your body. Vivation makes these subtle energies readily accessible.

How Vivation Affects Your Energy System

In order to deepen your understanding of The Five Elements, you can think of your body as an energy system. There exist many types of energy in the body, and many different models for explaining them. Most such models are derived from Eastern systems of physiology and medicine, from the realms of yoga, meditation and acupuncture. In this chapter I present a physical explanation of how Vivation works, using a minimum of technical language. (Please note, however, that you do not need to fully comprehend this explanation in order to get all the benefits of Vivation.)

In this explanation I use three concepts, derived from yoga, that you may or may not have heard of. These are *prana* and *apana*, which are energies of the body, and the *nadis*, which are the energy channels through which prana and apana flow.

Prana can be thought of as the energy of aliveness, the energy that builds and organizes the cells and tissues of the body. Prana is the energy you experience when you go for a walk in nature, when you eat fresh fruits and vegetables, when you take a deep breath of ocean breeze.

Apana is the energy your body uses for sending anything out of the body, for eliminating waste and toxins, for regulating growth in cells and tissues. You have a vivid experience of apana when you overeat or when you drink alcohol excessively. That's because your body has to generate more apana to eliminate the excess. Apana is not waste, but the energy your body uses to eliminate waste. Apana is not carbon dioxide. It is what your body uses to eliminate carbon dioxide.

The nadis are the pathways for the movement of prana and apana. The acupuncture meridians are probably the best known nadis, but the acupuncture meridians branch out and connect all the cells of the body together as one unit. The nadis trace both the nervous system and circulatory system, as well as having their own pathways.

Good health requires a proper balance of prana and apana throughout the organism. Life itself can be thought of as the dynamic dance between prana and apana. Everything influences the flow of prana and apana through your nadis: what you do, what you eat, what you think, other people in your environment, nearby electrical equipment, your posture, the weather—literally *everything*.

Energy

The system of nadis in the body are continuously adjusting the flow of prana and apana in order to stay in balance and respond appropriately to the environment. You may think of this as a conscious, self-regulating electrical system of energy in which the electrical resistance (and thus the flow of electricity) is in a continuous state of change throughout the system. For a few seconds, the flow of prana may be increased through your chest and arms, then for a few seconds, a surge of apana might begin in your lungs and extend up your throat, then your entire spinal cord might light up with a simultaneous downward surge of prana and upward surge of apana. All of this may occur without your having any conscious awareness of it.

Understand that this dance of energy happens both in response to your environment and in order to give you control over your environment. Understand also that these energy fluctuations occur both in response to the external world, other drivers on the road for instance, and your internal world, like remembering something your mother once said to you.

Emotions, understood from this perspective, are patterns of energy within the overall energy flow. The reason you are able to feel anger in your chest, or sadness in your face, is because these emotions change the flow of energy in these parts of your body. Each different thing you think about produces a different pattern of energy in your body.

The network of nadis is intricate throughout the body, but particularly intricate within the brain. The interconnection of nadis in the brain is even richer and more complex than the synaptic connections within the central nervous system. Understood energetically, your mind, your personality, your dreams, your suffering, and your expressions are all produced by subtle changes in the flow of prana and apana through your nadis. But remember, none of this is localized only in the brain: every thought, conscious or unconscious, produces waves of energy throughout your entire body.

To understand the technical aspects of how Vivation works, it is helpful to understand the energetic relationship between the mind and the body. All of your senses (sight, hearing, touch, taste, smell, etc.) operate through dynamic changes in the flow of prana and apana. When you listen to one kind of music, you get a different flow of energy than when you listen to another kind. When you watch television you get a different flow of energy than when you look at a delicate orchid. Similar differences in the flow of energy occur in response to internal experiences. When, in your mind's eye, you remember a purring cat, you get a totally different pattern of energy than when you remember driving past a highway accident.

Everything produces its own distinct pattern of energy within you. Each separate thing, tangible or intangible, each distinct part of each thing, each interaction between different parts of your experience, all produce distinct patterns of energy within you.

You, yourself, play a huge role in how each experience produces a pattern of energy within your body. How any particular thing affects you depends on your interpretation of it. If you put two people in a room with a cat, and one of the people likes cats and the other doesn't, the two people will have totally different patterns of energy in response to the same cat.

Whenever you experience something, you get a *pattern of energy* in your body. When you make something wrong, that is, when you respond to something as though it *should* be different from how it actually is, then you experience the pattern of energy you get as unpleasant. In fact, that is the definition of *unpleasantness*: the feeling produced by something you are making wrong.

Suppression

When you feel unpleasantness, you naturally do something in response. If you are like most people, your usual response to unpleasantness is *suppression*: trying to escape. What I suggest you do, however, whenever you can, is to focus on the unpleasant feeling and use Vivation to integrate it. (I'll tell you how to do this later. That, after all, is the whole point of this book.) If you integrate the feeling, you will immediately feel better and take effective action if any is needed. But that's not what people usually do. Most people respond to unpleasantness by suppressing their feelings, which, of course, only makes matters worse. There are many ways of suppressing feelings, but in general all forms of suppression fall into two categories: *reduction of awareness* (alcohol, watching television, withdrawing into work) and *control* (yelling, plotting, manipulating). These two general categories of suppression are closely related to one another and produce approximately the same effect energetically—reduction of consciousness and reduction of the flow of energy in the parts of the body affected by the pattern of energy. Getting angry and yelling at someone might seem superficially like an increase of energy in the feeling, but it is not. Instead it is channeling the energy from the area of discomfort into a pattern of energy that is more comfortable. The classic example is a man who initially feels saddened and hurt by his wife's behavior, but immediately masks that uncomfortable feeling with the more comfortable feeling of anger.

Suppression does not cause the feeling to go away. Obviously it cannot do so because what you are making wrong continues to exist, and the negative context itself continues to be there until you finally integrate it. Suppression only withdraws consciousness from the pattern of energy, so that the pattern of energy continues at the unconscious level, and you move on with less awareness of your energy system. The negative context also continues, but it operates from the unconscious level. Over a period of time, layer after layer of suppressed make-wrongs build up in the mind and body. This produces increasing unpleasantness, withdrawal of consciousness from the body, and a narrowing of what can be accepted and enjoyed in life.

Vivation directly counteracts this downward spiral. Each of The Five Elements plays an essential role in integration. All Five Elements are necessary in order to have integration. Whenever all Five Elements are present, integration happens. Whenever integration has not yet happened, it can be brought about by strengthening one or more of The Five Elements.

The First Element is Circular Breathing. This is breathing in a way that enhances the energetic connections within the body and re-energizes the patterns of energy that have been suppressed. Skillful Circular Breathing makes it possible to develop an energy-level rapport with a suppressed pattern of make-wrong, so that it is both easier to focus on it and easier to relate to it in a positive way.

The Second Element is Complete Relaxation. This eliminates the resistance to the feeling that has kept it suppressed. Make-wrong is always a constriction. Integration is always a relaxation.

The Third Element is Awareness in Detail. This is the reconnection of consciousness with a pattern of energy that has been suppressed. You cannot integrate something without being aware of it. The easiest way (in fact the only way) to integrate something deeply and thoroughly is by being aware of it at the feeling level.

The Fourth Element is Integration into Ecstasy. This is the re-embracing of something you had previously made wrong. Simple receptivity to the possibility that there might be something good about what you've been making wrong, or the recognition that your feeling about something is not infinitely unpleasant, is sufficient to achieve integration.

The Fifth Element is Do Whatever You Do—Willingness is Enough. This allows you to take your attention off the process and put it on the feeling in your body. You do not need special circumstances in order to integrate something and you do not need to do anything right. If you are willing to integrate, that willingness is all you really need, and if you know it is all you need, you'll achieve integration much more easily.

All make-wrong leads to suppression. In fact make-wrong itself is a form of suppression, since it is suppression of the knowledge of the good available in something. All Five Elements are necessary in order to completely undo suppression. If any one of them is missing, the other four are insufficient.

The next five chapters of this book go into each one of The Five Elements in great detail. With each Element, I explain its essence, why it is important, background information you need in order to understand it, how to apply it during a session, and how to cultivate greater skill with it.

In these chapters I emphasize thoroughness rather than simplicity. You'll be pleased to know that you do not need to keep all this information in mind during your session. The chapter immediately following the chapters on The Five Elements explains how to keep your application of the internal skill of Vivation absolutely simple during your sessions. It explains how to maintain all Five Elements continuously by only focusing on one thing at a time.

The Five Elements convey a tremendous depth and breadth of understanding. They not only teach a person how to Vive but also direct a person toward an *integrative way of life*. The Five Elements provide enduring and profound guidance for living a life of continuously expanding love.

CHAPTER 4

The First Element Of Vivation

CIRCULAR BREATHING

You can go without food or water for days or weeks, but you can only go without air for a few minutes. Prana, the life force energy in the body, comes from many sources: sunlight, food, water, air and others. But air is, by far, the most important source of prana.

Circular Breathing results in complete circuits of energy in the body—a balancing of prana and apana. Besides being the healthiest way to breathe in general, Circular Breathing provides many specific benefits for integrating feelings with Vivation. Essentially, it supports all the other Elements. It supports the Second Element because a pulse of relaxation goes through the entire body with each exhale. It supports the Third Element because it reenlivens the feelings that have been suppressed. It supports the Fourth Element because it feels good. It supports the Fifth Element, because the energy connection puts your spirit in the driver's seat. Circular Breathing brings feelings out of suppression and makes it easy to embrace them. It provides a tonic to every cell of the body. Circular Breathing is the most natural way to breathe: most babies (and all cats!) keep their breathing Circular a majority of the time.

Circular Breathing unites your conscious mind with your unconscious, and brings your spirit into your body. It makes you aware of the play of creativity going on throughout your entire being at all times. It balances the energy in your body and highlights the areas where a resistance can be embraced.

Why is Circular Breathing so important? Your body is more than flesh and blood. Your body is a dynamic energy system. The energy in your body moves in waves, just as everything in nature does. The point of the First Element is to breathe in a way that develops waves of energy in your body that harmonize with the waves of energy in your feelings. Most people cannot connect deeply with their body's wisdom without good Circular Breathing skills.

Circular Breathing, used well, does not change the way you feel, it enables you to feel what you already feel in greater detail. The breathing doesn't give you a better feeling than you already have, it connects you more consciously with the ecstasy that is already within you naturally all the time. Circular Breathing facilitates you in integrating feelings that you have been making wrong, and doing so *does* make you feel different—a whole lot better! But the best way to use Circular Breathing in order to have as much integration as possible is to just use the breathing to help you focus on the feeling, not to try to change it.

Your path to mastering the First Element begins with learning how to do Circular Breathing, and ultimately takes you to the ability to make fine adjustments in the breathing continuously in order to maintain rapport with the ever-shifting feelings that come up during the session.

Circular Breathing is a continuous breath, with no pauses anywhere, so your consciousness is also continuous. It emphasizes the inhale, taking in the perfection of the moment. The exhale is completely relaxed—not controlled in any way—so your entire being can relax. To assist your concentration on the feelings in your body, imagine that each inhale enters your body through the sensation that is strongest in the moment. This enables you to draw the feeling into your awareness at the same time you draw the breath into your body.

How To Do Circular Breathing

Circular Breathing is any kind of breathing that has all of the following three characteristics:

1. The inhale and the exhale are connected together with no pauses anywhere.

2. The exhale is completely relaxed and not controlled at all.

3. If the inhale comes in through the nose, then the exhale also goes out through the nose. If the inhale comes in through the mouth, then the exhale also goes out through the mouth.

Circular Breathing is sometimes slow, other times fast; sometimes full, and other times shallow; you can do it in the upper part of the lungs or the lower, breathing through either nose or mouth. The continuity and connectedness of the breathing are essential, as is the complete relaxation of the exhale. All other factors are adjusted, depending on what's happening in the Vivation session at the moment.

Circular Breathing sends high-amplitude, slow-frequency waves of energy through your body. Within a few minutes of starting Circular Breathing, you become more aware of your body as an energy system. Circular Breathing works together with the other Elements to empower you to embrace emotions you've been resisting, which have been limiting your enjoyment of life and your effective, creative action.

The breathing enables you to feel the aliveness streaming through your body, including through the parts of your body that you had been avoiding noticing because of suppressed emotions. The waves of energy created by Circular Breathing produce a pleasurable pulsing throughout your body that soothes and relaxes your spirit at the same time it heightens your awareness.

Adjusting the Breathing Rhythm

Breathing more fully sends higher amplitude waves through the body, resulting in greater intensity of sensation. If the feelings are not vivid enough to hold your attention, breathe more fully. But the goal is detailed awareness, not intensity—if the feelings are too intense you have less detailed awareness. When the feelings are more intense than you prefer, take smaller breaths.

Breathing faster speeds up the massaging pulses of energy moving through your body, enhancing your awareness of the dynamic dance of aliveness within the feeling you're exploring. Some feelings are easier for people to embrace than others. When feelings come up that seem uncomfortable, speed up the breathing. When you feel the energy dancing within the grief or pain, you will be able to embrace it easily. When bliss or other pleasant feelings are coming up, you breathe slowly, to drink in the delicious details of the feeling. This is what people do naturally. When standing on top of a mountain taking in the beautiful vista, people naturally breathe slowly and fully. When they stub their toe on a sofa they breathe fast and shallowly.

You can focus your attention on a feeling in the upper part of your body more easily when you are breathing in the upper part of your lungs. When the strongest feeling is in the lower part of your body, you can explore that more easily by breathing in the lower part of your lungs. If you simply remember to pull the breath in through the strongest feeling, you automatically place the breath correctly.

Whether to breathe through the nose or through the mouth is a matter of preference—whichever feels better is better. In Circular Breathing we do not inhale through one and exhale through the other, because doing so breaks up the focused movement of energy through the body and diverts attention from the feeling that's coming up.

The Three Energy States

There are three main combinations of the speed and the volume that it's useful for us to go over. These correspond to the Three Energy States. The Three Energy States have to do with how you are responding to your experience. In any given moment of your life (not just during Vivation) you will always be in either Bliss, Unconsciousness or Discomfort. You are in a state of Bliss when you are feeling the feelings in your body in detail and enjoying them. You are in a state of Unconsciousness when you are not paying attention to the feelings in your body. You are in a state of Discomfort when you are feeling the feelings in your body and making them wrong.

In day-to-day life, outside of Vivation sessions, my experience is that more than 90% of people are in a state of unconsciousness. Next most common for the masses of people is discomfort. And less than 1% of all people are in bliss. During Vivation sessions, where people are intentionally cultivating both their awareness and their capacity for enjoyment, people are in each of the three Energy States about equally. In other words, if you have thirty people Viving in a room simultaneously, half an hour into the session you'll probably have about ten people in each of the three Energy States. At the end of the session you'll probably have thirty people in Bliss!

Helpful Breathing Rhythms

For each of the three Energy States a different main breathing rhythm is most helpful. When people are in bliss they get the most integration breathing slowly and fully. When they're in unconsciousness they get the most integration breathing fast and fully. When they're in discomfort they get the most integration breathing fast and shallowly.

Helpful Breathing Rhythms

ENERGY STATE	TYPE OF BREATHING
1. Bliss	Sustain with *slow and full*
2. Unconsciousness	Overcome with *fast and full*
3. Discomfort	Handle with *fast and shallow*

Slow and full

Use slow full Circular Breathing at the very beginning of your session and when you're having an easy time blissing out on every detail of your experience. The fullness of slow full Circular Breathing makes the patterns of energy emerge more strongly from the background feeling of your body. The slowness of slow full Circular Breathing makes it especially easy to focus your attention on the details of what's coming up. When you're using slow full Circular Breathing, don't struggle to get the last possible cubic centimeter of air into your lungs; simply fill your lungs until they're as full as they're going to be and still be comfortable. Also don't try to get all the air out of your lungs; instead just let the exhale go as far as it will with relaxation alone. Make sure you don't pause at the end of the exhale; it's better to err on the side of starting the inhale too soon instead of too late. If your inhale feels kind of jerky then speed it up just slightly and that will give you the nice, smooth draw that is desirable on the inhale.

Fast and full

Use fast and full Circular Breathing whenever you experience feelings that tend to take you out of your body—sleepiness for example. The large volume of air keeps you in your body and the speed gives you a physiological reminder of the pleasure of being alive, which helps you integrate the unconsciousness. In order to make the fast and full Circular Breathing work effectively it is necessary to focus directly on the feeling of sleepiness. If the feeling is manifesting mainly in your head, which is usual, the fast and full Circular Breathing will be best taken into the uppermost part of your lungs. When you become aware of the sleepiness in detail and you accept it into your over-all sense of pleasure and well-being, it integrates just like anything else. Fast and full Circular Breathing is not hyperventilation. Fast and full breathing that is not properly Circular might very well cause hyperventilation. To counteract this make relaxation a higher priority than speed. If your body tells you it wants to slow down or breathe a little less, then *do* slow down or breathe a little less. If fast and full Circular Breathing seems like hard work, it's because it reminds you of how you breathe when you are doing hard work. Breathing itself is not hard work. When you integrate the emotions you have about hard work, fast and full Circular Breathing will always feel fine from that point on.

Fast and shallow

Use fast and shallow Circular Breathing when you have feelings that are both intense and uncomfortable. The shallowness of fast and shallow Circular Breathing reduces the intensity of the feeling. The speed of fast and shallow Circular Breathing gives you a physiological reminder of the pleasure of being alive, which makes it easier to integrate the painful sensation. Fast and shallow Circular Breathing works both on physical pain and on emotional pain. In order to make fast and shallow Circular Breathing work efficiently it is necessary to focus directly on the emotion or sensation that seems painful.

Mastery over the First Element means fine-tuning the breathing rhythm with precision. In other words, you not only want to get the right one of the three main breathing rhythms, you actually want to tune the breathing rhythm to the pattern of energy manifesting in your body at the present moment. Please note: you will get a huge, positive result from Vivation even before you learn how to fine-tune your Circular Breathing. After you've had a few sessions you will naturally want to learn how to do this fine-tuning in order to gain mastery over the process.

I like to explain fine-tuning the breathing rhythm with an analogy. Imagine you're sitting in a sound studio and you've got a dial that allows you to adjust the pitch (frequency) of a tone. Imagine that you are also listening to another tone over which you have no control. You can adjust the pitch of the tone over which you do have control to form any harmonic resonance you wish with the tone over which you do not have control. You can make the tone you're controlling a perfect fifth higher or an octave lower or anything you want. You don't need an oscilloscope to do this. If you're adjusting your tone to be an octave lower, when you get close, but not quite on the right frequency, it won't sound good. But when you get to exactly the right tone, suddenly it sounds just right, and even feels just right. The feeling in your body in the present moment is analogous to the tone over which you do not have control. (In Vivation you never want to control the feeling that is coming up.) Your breathing rhythm is analogous to the tone over which you do have control. You want to pay very close attention to the feeling and playfully adjust the breathing rhythm, a little faster, then a little slower, until you get the breathing rhythm just right. This is actually quite easy to do. As the feeling changes in subtle ways from moment to moment, you will want to adjust the breathing rhythm subtly with each breath. With a little practice this will virtually take care of itself, as long as you continue to focus your attention on the feeling.

The Breathing Range Exercise

In this exercise you experiment to find the full range of breathing rhythms that you can do comfortably.

Adjustments to the breathing are subtle. The "three" breathing rhythms are really infinitely many, because there are unlimited possibilities within each of the three main ones. Here's an exercise you can try right now to experience the subtleties within the range of possible breathing rhythms. Since the instructions are simple, I suggest reading them first, then closing your eyes and doing the exercise.

During this entire exercise, don't let your breathing pause for even a moment. Keep your breathing connected and Circular throughout.

Very important! Hyperventilation (dizziness) is NOT a normal part of this exercise. If you start to hyperventilate or feel overly dizzy, STOP: You're not doing the breathing correctly—you should see a Vivation Professional before continuing. Keep your exhale completely relaxed (neither speeded up nor slowed down) throughout this exercise. If you keep your exhale completely relaxed, you will not hyperventilate even with the fastest and fullest Circular Breathing rhythm, but you may need lessons from a Vivation Professional in order to learn to relax the exhale.

1. First do the slowest, fullest Circular Breathing that you can.

2. Now keep the breathing full and gradually speed it up, until eventually you are doing the fastest and fullest Circular Breathing that you can.

3. Now keep the breathing fast and gradually take smaller and smaller inhales, until eventually you are doing the fastest and shallowest Circular Breathing that you can.

An important concept in learning to master Circular Breathing is the idea of receiving the energy from the pattern of energy. Everything you feel is made of energy that you need. Obviously every feeling is made of your life force energy. Make-wrong and suppression cause the energy in the body to become separated, compartmentalized. With each inhale you want to focus on taking the energy that is within the strongest feeling back into your conscious energy system. Doing so not only harmonizes and unifies your energy. It also benefits your mind. Whatever the feeling is about becomes transformed from something you resist to something you embrace and utilize. This is the essence of integration.

Hyperventilation

Circular Breathing does not cause hyperventilation. Even if you were to hyperventilate, you would not be harmed by it. (Incidentally, you can't hurt yourself by hyperventilating for the same reason you can't hurt yourself by holding your breath. Your brain will adjust your breathing automatically to maintain the oxygen balance that it requires.) If you keep the exhale completely relaxed, you will get no signs or symptoms of hyperventilation even using the fastest and fullest Circular Breathing rhythms. Some people, when they are first learning Circular Breathing, do go through some hyperventilation. The Vivation Professional will help such a person learn to relax the exhale and integrate the feelings that are associated with this incidental hyperventilation.

Tetany

Sometimes if people hyperventilate while learning to do Circular Breathing they experience a harmless condition called "tetany," in which the hands or another part of the body tighten up. Tetany is interesting to experience and not uncomfortable unless the Viver struggles against it. It lasts briefly and people only experience it within their first few sessions, if at all. Most people never experience any tetany, even in the beginning, provided they receive adequate instruction from their Vivation Professional.

Tingling

Something that people usually do experience is tingling in different parts of their body. Tingling is unrelated to hyperventilation and tetany. When people have tetany they almost always have tingling as well, but most people have tingling without ever having any tetany. Tingling and tetany are caused by totally different things. Tetany is caused by a build-up of apana that results from controlling the exhale. Tingling is caused by a greater circulation of energy than the person is accustomed to. Tingling with Circular Breathing is analogous to the tingling experienced when you've been sitting in a position that cuts off circulation to your leg, so your leg falls asleep. While it's asleep it doesn't feel like anything; but when you straighten out your leg and the circulation is restored, you experience "pins and needles" tingling as your leg is on its way back to normal awareness. Obviously once your leg has its normal circulation and awareness restored, it doesn't tingle anymore. The same thing happens with tingling in Vivation, although it's the circulation of prana, rather than the circulation of blood, that is involved.

Circulation of prana is reduced by suppression. Circular Breathing undoes the suppression and renews the normal circulation of energy. During the transition period, tingling is experienced. Once normal circulation of energy has been restored, the tingling ceases, and the person simply experiences more awareness and energy in the affected part of the body than they did before. Tingling happens at different times in different parts of the body.

Generally tingling happens in a person's Vivation sessions for the first year or two that they are doing Vivation. After that, circulation of energy is normalized sufficiently for the added energy from Circular Breathing to feel simply like a flow of energy instead of like tingling.

Tips for Improving Your Use of Circular Breathing

Your suppression makes you want to breathe less. As a general rule, breathe more fully than you think you want to during your Vivation sessions.

The aforementioned Breathing Range Exercise is useful in many different ways. It's a great way to start your Vivation sessions, since it immediately increases the flexibility of your breathing. It's a great thing to do first thing in the morning and for short restorative breaks several times during the day. If you do it thoroughly, meaning that you explore all the possible breathing rhythms in between the extremes, every cell of your body will be harmonized, because each part of your body has a natural resonance with a different breathing rhythm.

If you find that one of the three main breathing rhythms is difficult for you, practice that particular one until it becomes comfortable. Similarly, if you find that you are only comfortable breathing through your nose, practice breathing through your mouth and vice versa. If you only like breathing in the upper part of your lungs, then practice breathing in the lower part of your lungs until you use that comfortably. You want your breathing to be as flexible as possible.

Besides Circular Breathing there are literally hundreds of other breathing techniques, each of which produces a different result. (Integrating emotions is a result unique to Vivation.) You will gain a greater mastery over Circular Breathing if you learn as much as you can about how breathing affects consciousness. I recommend experimenting with all different forms of pranayama (Indian yoga breathing) and chi gung (Chinese Taoist breathing, related to acupuncture). Whenever possible, study with competent teachers.

With practice you can learn to play your breathing like an instrument, making beautiful music in concert with the feelings your body presents to you.

CHAPTER 5

The Second Element of Vivation

COMPLETE RELAXATION

During Vivation you relax your mind and body as much as possible, and then continue to relax them more and more throughout your session. Restlessness of the mind and body is an essential component of suppression. Suppression requires continuous effort. Suppression always involves using part of your energy to hold back another part of your energy. In terms of the mind, suppression means giving part of your mind the task of preventing you from thinking about something. Make-wrong itself requires effort. Reality is the way it is. Integration is simply allowing it to be the way it is. Make-wrong is insisting that it should be different. Wasted effort! No matter how hard you insist, it's still the way it is.

Vivation is not a cathartic process. Cathartic processes are based on the erroneous concept that suppressed emotions are something toxic that must be "gotten out." In cathartic processes people typically do a lot of screaming, acting out, beating on pillows, etc. The desire to get rid of an emotion is exactly the same thing as make-wrong and suppression. Cathartic processes often make people even more afraid of their emotions than they were before.

Vivation is an integrative process. In Vivation we know that suppressed emotions only need to be experienced in detail and embraced. In fact, we know that you can never exactly get rid of an emotion. Even if you could, doing so would be undesirable. Your emotions all exist to create benefit for you. When you integrate an emotion you keep the energy and benefit of the emotion, and by embracing it, you drop the negativity. This leaves you with positive emotions, unified energy, mental clarity and a more perfect world.

Negativity is created by resistance to something in life being the way it is. The proper goal of all personal development work is the full embracing of reality. Here's the essential point of how Vivation works: *The resistance to the emotion is exactly the same as the resistance to the thing itself you have that emotion about.* If you drop your resistance to the emotion, which is what you do when you Vive, you simultaneously drop your resistance to something important in your life. After that you will have a positive relationship to the same thing you were negative about. The easiest way to do this is to focus your attention on feeling the emotion you don't like and relax completely in the presence of the feeling, not trying to get rid of it, letting go of even hoping it will change.

All the Elements of Vivation depend on Complete Relaxation. And all Five Elements support you in relaxing more and more.

Expressing or acting out emotions is not part of Vivation. Watching from the outside, Vivation sessions might look rather boring to someone who's not trained in what to watch for. Superficially, people having Vivation sessions just look like they are relaxing and breathing. Of course an experienced Vivation Professional sees outward signs of the rich adventure that is going on inside the Viver! If you know what to look for, Vivation sessions are very exciting to watch, even though they do not involve a lot of theater. The most dramatic results usually come from the least dramatic-looking sessions.

Gentleness

Gentleness is extremely important in Vivation. Contrary to the cathartic model, no dynamite is needed to blast through layers of suppression, even for extremely suppressed people. Suppression simply doesn't work that well! If you just relax while giving attention to the feelings in your body, you discover your most important emotions right on the surface. The gentleness of Vivation makes the Viver feel much safer, and with greater safety comes greater willingness to allow feelings to surface. Gentleness reduces suppression much more effectively than screaming, confrontation, sleep deprivation and drama ever could. People have too much harshness in their lives already. They do not need even more of it in the form of "therapy"! Vivation is gentler than what people usually do in their day-to-day lives. Giving loving attention to the feelings in your body is much gentler than suppressing feelings. Vivation is the skill of being nice to yourself.

The Meaning of Relaxation

Here are some points about the meaning of relaxation that will add some clarity about how to apply the Second Element. When muscles relax, they become longer and softer. Joints become loser. When energy channels relax, they open. When the mind relaxes, it becomes quieter and less controlled. Relaxation is related to receptivity and is the opposite of control. Relaxation is about experiencing and is the opposite of doing. Relaxation is about allowing to happen and is the opposite of trying to produce a result. When you're relaxed, your perception of your body becomes more internal and three-dimensional. With relaxation your spirit reveals itself and the natural ecstasy of existence itself becomes apparent.

Relaxation is continuous during Vivation, and a pulse of relaxation goes through the entire body with every exhale. With every exhale, just let everything drop. Let go of holding yourself up and let the present moment itself support your body.

Don't do anything at all with your mind during Vivation. Don't try to remember anything. Don't try to figure anything out. Don't try to solve any problems. Don't try to produce any results. Don't try to think positive thoughts. Just let your mind run all by itself without any participation from you, rather like hearing a neighbor's radio playing in the distance. When your mind has an insight, just thank your mind for being so brilliant and go back to focusing on your feeling awareness. Give your mind a completely free reign. Let your thoughts surprise you.

A principle of the Second Element can be illustrated well by three strange sentences:

#1 *Let every itch be its own scratch.* This does not mean you'll spoil your session if you scratch an itch. What it means is that if you don't scratch the itch, but instead just focus on it, inhale through it, and apply The Five Elements, it will feel like the itch scratches itself.

#2 *Let every ache be its own massage.* Very often a complete Vivation session feels like you just received a full body massage. In fact, during Vivation you are massaging yourself from the inside using your breath and your loving attention.

#3 *Let every desire be its own satisfaction.* Every make-wrong carries with it a desire. Very often these desires will become active during Vivation sessions. Most people think that if you have a desire you have a choice between two options: either satisfy it, or try and forget about it (that is, *suppress* it). Vivation provides a third and superior option: Integrate it. Focus on what the desire feels like and let everything relax. You can use Vivation to quit smoking or break any kind of bad habit, by simply using Vivation to integrate the feelings that come up and relaxing instead of taking action on the desire.

Vivation Posture

In general, we recommend that the Viver get into one comfortable position and keep relaxing in that position, without much movement or talking throughout the whole session. Lying on one's back, legs uncrossed, palms up at the sides is often best for people who are not having difficulties with unconsciousness. This is the position that supports the Second Element the best for most people. Sitting comfortably, either in a chair or on the floor, always works well, and for someone going through unconsciousness, is much better than lying down. Other positions can also be suitable, provided they facilitate relaxation and full breathing.

Sometimes a Viver's first awareness of a pattern of energy emerging from suppression is awareness of an area of the body that will not relax. If you find that happening in your session, focus on the feeling and relax *about* it. Explore it with your consciousness and let go of your desire to control it or even relax it. Don't try to relax it. Accept it exactly as it is.

Circular Breathing causes an increase in the flow of energy in your body and you can either relax into it and let it heal you or you can attempt to resist it and have the effort of resisting it make you more tense.

Relaxation is always an essential component of every integration, because at the moment of integration, energy that has been made wrong and held away is reaccepted, and the very cells of the body drop their struggle against it.

Subtlety and Drama

Another important point about the Second Element can be illustrated through a careful exploration of the concepts of subtlety and drama. Every feeling can be integrated when it is at a *subtle* level of manifestation in the body. No feeling ever needs to become intense to be integrated. The feeling needs to be experienced in detail, but detailed awareness is something completely different from intensity. Listening attentively to your stereo is completely different from turning the volume all the way up.

Drama means acting out a feeling rather than relaxing and integrating it. Outward expressions, such as screaming, are almost always drama, but not quite always. Sometimes a scream comes out completely spontaneously. Application of The Second Element means that you neither try to hold the scream back, nor do you voluntarily push the scream. If it would take more effort not to scream than to scream, you are better off allowing the scream to come out. Weeping is usually not drama, and is usually to be encouraged. However, sometimes people focus more on making sure that everyone knows how miserable they are than on feeling their feelings. This is drama and should not be encouraged.

Laughter is common during Vivation and is not drama when it is spontaneous. You will sometimes find people who are laughing instead of feeling, however, or who are using laughter simply to get attention, which is obviously not the best way to integrate emotions.

In Vivation, patience really is a virtue, because it makes it possible to relax and focus on the present moment rather then trying to rush a result. Integration develops patience and patience develops integration.

There are some parts of the body where people habitually remain tense even when they are trying to relax and Vive. This varies from person to person, but in general, care should be given to keeping the throat, jaw and forehead relaxed. Any sounds coming from the vocal cords are a sign that the throat is not relaxed. Moaning, humming and other vocalizations are unproductive during sessions.

Talking during Vivation sessions should be limited to the amount that is necessary to keep the session progressing. The Viver does not need to tell the coach a running commentary on everything going on in the session. The Viver does not need to explain great ideas that come up and does not need to talk about memories. Obviously it is OK for the Viver to say anything at any time. Asking for a blanket if you're feeling cold is obviously a good idea. But generally talking should be before the session or after the session, not during.

Tips for Improving Your Skill with The Second Element

Decide what you personally find relaxing. This is somewhat different for different people. Listening to music, taking baths, reading, walking, playing with your cats. Do more of whatever is relaxing for you.

Get bodywork. Almost all kinds of bodywork improve the Second Element. These include massage, Trager, Body Harmony, Rolfing, and many others.

Self-hypnosis helps many people learn to relax.

Almost all kinds of meditation help a person learn to relax.

Spending time in nature is helpful, not just for the Second Element but really for all Five Elements. In Vivation you are spending time with nature inside yourself. Spending time with nature outside yourself will help you become accustomed to nature within yourself.

Soaking in natural hot springs is particularly good at supporting the Second Element.

Learning to avoid or reduce stressful activities and situations is also important for developing ability with the Second Element. If the Second Element is your weakest, then avoid coffee and other stimulants. Avoid vexatious people. Do everything you can to reduce the stress involved in your work, even if it means changing careers.

Vivation itself is the best thing you can do to learn to relax!

CHAPTER 6

The Third Element of Vivation

AWARENESS IN DETAIL

Even if it's true that miracles occur every day, the miracle you're closest to is the dance of your own spirit within your body. When people learn Vivation, a whole new universe opens to their exploration. Apart from all the benefits you can achieve through Vivation, the entertainment value alone makes Vivation more worthwhile than practically any other activity! In that respect Vivation is a bit like driving. Why learn to drive? Well, there are all sorts of practical benefits, but an even better reason is because it's fun! Vivation is more fun than driving (and makes driving more fun). And, yes, integrating feelings has all sorts of practical benefits.

In order to integrate something, you must have a conscious connection with it. You simply cannot change your mind about something without knowing what you are changing your mind about. In Vivation you make this conscious connection at the feeling level.

The essence of the Third Element is feeling the present moment in as much detail as possible. This is a skill of receptivity and requires abandoning control over your feelings and letting your feelings come to you. During a Vivation session, you want to have the same amount of control over the feelings in your body as you have over a ballerina on a stage when you're in the audience. None. You simply want to give the feeling your maximum attention and enjoy its dance as much as possible.

You apply the Third Element by scanning through your feeling awareness of your body and locating the feeling that is most prominent in the present moment, then focusing your fullest possible attention on feeling that in as much detail as you can. Try to feel every cell that is affected by the pattern of energy.

When you feel the feeling in detail you always find that it changes in subtle ways from moment to moment. Continuously explore the feeling and the subtle changes, traveling around inside your body with your consciousness.

This is very simple, and yet it is impossible to do without the rest of the Elements. Similarly, all of the other Elements depend completely upon the Third. Awareness in Detail is extremely important because if you don't let any feelings come up you won't integrate any feelings.

The Third Element is an unusually natural thing to do. Whatever most asks for your attention is what you give the most attention to. It's really that simple, but it's not what most people do most of the time.

For somewhat more than half of all people learning Vivation, the Third Element is their weakest until they have had several Vivation sessions. This is partly due to the fact that people need some confidence in their own ability to integrate their feelings before they are willing to let them come up. Otherwise they will be afraid of being overwhelmed by the feelings coming out of suppression.

The other main reason people have trouble with the Third Element is that focusing on subtle changes within feelings in the body is just not what most people are accustomed to doing. I suspect that our modern society has externalized people's awareness more than ever before in history. This is especially a result of television, which gives us the expectation that external entertainment should always be available to us 24 hours a day, at the mere flick of a switch. People need retraining and practice to put their attention back inside themselves.

Another interesting point about society encouraging the externalization of attention, is that for anybody to control you they have to convince you that something else is more important than your feelings. If your attention is on your feelings, then you'll do what you know is right and not be so easily pushed and pulled by the whims of others! Vivation Professionals see this constantly with their clients. After just a few Vivation sessions, people just don't get controlled the same way by bosses, parents, spouses, advertisers, priests, governments, salesmen, and so on. And the converse is also true. Without knowing what they're doing, all the different individuals and institutions who want to control you encourage you constantly to make your own feelings a lower and lower priority. If you want to control someone, obviously your main competition is their own self-control.

Vivation moves us toward a society in which people's ethics, responsibility and sense of purpose come naturally from their own individual spirit, and not from the unconscious minds of a few authority figures. If you take the time to learn how to focus on the feelings in your body and follow them as they move within you, you will find a greater wisdom within yourself than you could ever possibly find externally.

I like to use an analogy for explaining how to transfer awareness to your feeling sense. If you go to a concert, all your senses are active but you especially tune in your hearing sense. It is possible to sit at the concert and be off in your thoughts so much that you don't even hear the music. There is skill involved in listening to music well. During Vivation all your senses are active but you especially focus on your feeling sense. When images or words come into your mind, that's fine, just notice how you feel about them.

Getting Less Mental

One of the great benefits of Vivation is that it makes people less mental. Most people go around thinking, thinking, thinking all day. This is way out of balance. The mind is obviously a wonderful tool for getting things done, but you want it to be your servant, not your master. Intuition, purpose, creativity, compassion, joy and spirituality do not come from the mind. If you want to develop these qualities, then you have to stop giving all your attention to your mind, and learn to pay more attention to your feelings. If you try to develop these qualities without getting more in touch with your feelings, you'll wind up with cheap substitutes that give no real satisfaction.

During Vivation, make no distinction between physical sensations and the feelings produced by emotions. In connection with Vivation, the word "feeling" means literally anything at all that you feel. It means the feeling of fear. It also means the feeling of tiredness. It means feeling worried. It also mean feeling awestruck by the grandeur of God. It means feeling like you drank too much coffee. It also means feeling an itchy mosquito bite. Anything you feel, in any sense of the word, "feel."

Emotions manifest physically in the body as feelings. For example, when someone is feeling angry what they actually feel in their body might be tightness in their jaw and arms, and heat in their face. Part of how people identify their emotions in day-to-day life is by the situation they're in. For example, while at work you might easily define a feeling in your body as *anger* partly because of the physical presence of your boss while you are having that feeling. If you are just relaxing in the presence of your Vivation Professional, and some anger starts coming out of suppression, you might not even identify it as being anger. You might just call it tightening in your jaw and arms and heat in your face. That's fine. You'll get just as much integration simply feeling the feeling in your body as you would if you identified it as anger. You'll get more integration by just focusing on the physical sensations, than by trying to figure out what to say to your boss!

It's fine if your session is completely physical. If your body selects purely physical feelings for your session, then that's what is most important for you to integrate. Your body is always right. But some of the time when you think you're having a purely physical session, what's actually going on is emotions.

Having a mental understanding of what's coming up during a Vivation session is completely worthless. Part of what's involved in developing mastery over the process is letting go of attachment to mentally understanding what is occurring. It's better to completely let go of your mind and only keep focusing more and more on your feeling sense.

Sometimes during Vivation you'll have a Technicolor movie of some incident from your past and you'll know exactly what the feeling is about. Sometimes you won't have a clue what the feeling is about. Other times, you'll think you know what the feelings are about, and you'll be wrong. All three of these work equally well.

Not only do you not need to understand the feeling, you do not even need to label or identify it. The feelings change rapidly and continuously, like water flowing in a stream. To label the feeling is like taking a snapshot of the stream. The snapshot fails to capture the movement. Labeling the feeling takes you out of the flow of feelings. In any moment your feelings are infinitely richer and more complex than can possibly be captured in words.

Feeling the feeling is everything. Understanding the feeling is nothing.

Do not use any form of mental process during your Vivation session. Specifically I want to mention affirmations, because often people who learn Vivation also use affirmations. Affirmations can be extremely effective tools for personal development, but not during Vivation sessions. Mentally saying affirmations to yourself during Vivation will just take your awareness away from your feelings. You wouldn't go to a concert and talk to yourself. (Or if you did, you wouldn't get as much from the music.) For exactly the same reason, do not say affirmations to yourself during your session.

It's very important in Vivation (and in life) not to be too careful about what you think. For example, being careful to think only positive thoughts simply makes the barrier between your conscious mind and your unconscious mind even thicker. You want your unconscious mind to tell you what it thinks. Whenever it gives you a negative thought, thank it for sharing with you! It is the negative thoughts that remain *unconscious* that you really need to be concerned with. During a Vivation session, welcome all negativity that arises and just keep focusing on the feeling it produces. Embracing that feeling will completely integrate the negativity, completely transforming it into positivity at the deepest level. You can't afford the luxury of suppressing a negative thought!

Trusting the Body

During Vivation, just focus on the feeling that's strongest in the present moment. You are much better off not trying to get to a more important feeling during a Vivation session. Just focus on whatever feeling is actually strongest in the present moment, even if that feeling seems very ordinary. Trust your body to present the right feeling at the right time. Your body knows better than your conscious mind does what's in your unconscious mind.

Here's an analogy: if you're digging a hole that's a meter deep, you don't start by taking out the scoop that's a meter below the surface first! You start with the shovel full that's actually on the surface. When that one's gone, you again take the scoop that's on the surface, and so on. Then pretty soon the shovel full that's one meter down will be on the surface and you'll take that one. It is exactly the same in Vivation. Your body knows what feeling to present to you in the present moment just as the earth knows what shovel full of dirt to present to you in the present moment.

One of the most important concepts in Vivation is that of "body leadership." Body leadership means allowing your body to present you with surprising feelings, allowing the feelings to take their own course through your completely relaxed body. Body leadership occurs when you pay close attention to the details within your feelings, without trying to control them in any way. You concentrate your full attention on your feeling sense, and just let your mind go. When you surrender to the leadership of your own body, your feelings take you on a healing adventure within yourself.

Staying in The Moment

During Vivation, only focus on your present-moment experience. This is the best way to clear any emotions left over from your past. I have an analogy to illustrate how this works: If you pack a lunch and go on a hike, when it's lunch time you don't have to go back to the moment when you packed your lunch in order to eat it. You have access to it better in the present moment. It's exactly the same with feelings. The past is over. All that matters about the past is what you're carrying with you from the past. If you're carrying it with you, you can have access to it better by focusing on what it feels like right now. Trying to go back to the past superimposes your imagination over the feeling, makes you more mental, and reduces your access to the real feeling. Staying in the present moment allows your body to present feelings to you in what it knows to be the optimum order.

When you have a memory come up during Vivation don't try to go back in your mind to the time the memory came from. Instead just focus on the feeling it's producing for you right now.

Surprise

Whenever you're focused on the present moment there is always an element of surprise. That's because you've never had a moment like this one before! Anytime you don't feel surprised, it's because of suppression. The more suppressed a person is the more things look to them as though they stay the same. This is one of the reasons why it's important not to try and control what comes up in the session. Always let your body surprise you with the feelings that it knows to be most important.

There's Always a Feeling

There is no such thing as nothing coming up in a session. When people think there's nothing coming up, it's because they are looking for something other than what they are actually feeling, looking for something that isn't there. If your mind is saying there's nothing coming up, then notice how you feel about that (*frustrated*, for example) then focus on that feeling.

Sometimes the strongest feeling in the present moment might just be the feeling of sitting in the chair, or the feeling of your clothes against your skin, or the feeling of air passing in and out of your nose. That's fine. If that's the strongest feeling then focus on that.

There are two main ways to make a feeling stand out more from the background feeling of your body. One is to breathe more fully. The other is to focus on maximizing your enjoyment of the present moment; doing so makes anything you're not enjoying stand out in sharper contrast.

Distraction

During Vivation nothing is ever a distraction. Whatever seems like it might be a distraction is producing a feeling in your body. If you just focus on that feeling, then the "distraction" will be actually helping you stay with your feelings. It is best to be aware of "external" things, rather than try to screen them out. Obviously you get activated by what happens in your environment, so the traffic noise, or a telephone ringing, or the sound of people talking are important parts of a Vivation session when they happen. Sometimes during a session you might feel angry at the sounds of other people Viving nearby, or even at a suggestion made by your Vivation Professional. When that happens, feel the anger in detail, and accept that it is your own anger that has gotten activated, not something done "wrong" by another person.

By feeling the present moment in sufficient detail, you not only find out which suppressed emotions have been running your life, you also discover the benefit, the blessing, the pleasure that they contain. All feelings are made of spiritual, healing energy. If you just feel the feeling in enough detail you'll find the hidden treasure within the feeling, and experience integration.

Vivation cannot bring up any feelings you don't already have. It will absolutely bring up every feeling you do have. It then takes you beyond the initial experience, into wonder, wisdom, and understanding. Embracing an emotion with detailed awareness is infinitely different from the ordinary experience of emotion that people have when they try to control, escape, and avoid.

Suppose you have some fear within you left over from a past experience. Then you might have a Vivation session in which you experience fear vividly—but the experience doesn't stop there. Very quickly, within seconds, Vivation moves you through to the integration of the fear, to a place beyond judgment, where the energy that had been trapped is free to contribute to your unconditional love and your knowledge of what you need.

Infinite Varieties of Bliss

I have personally led more than 10,000 people through Vivation sessions. I still find it astonishing that each individual who tries Vivation has a completely different experience than everyone else! Everybody completes each session in a state of peace, because the technique develops peace with whatever comes up. But "what comes up" is completely different for each person, and different for the same person from session to session! Every Vivation session you have is different from all your other sessions, because once you've integrated something, it no longer needs to come up again.

How to Manage Your Mind During Vivation Sessions

Even though Vivation is about the feelings in your body, not about the thoughts in your mind, your mind will keep thinking throughout your session. Vivation does not have a goal of stopping your mind. What you want to do is allow your mind to do anything at all, and simply keep focusing on your feeling awareness.

We all access our internal world visually (through pictures), verbally (through words), and kinesthetically (through feelings). These "internal senses" are all going on continuously. Different people have different habits regarding which of these they pay the most attention to.

Regardless of how you usually access your internal world, during Vivation you want to focus on your *feeling* sense. If you are primarily visual, just keep focusing on how you *feel* about the different pictures that come up for you. If you are primarily verbal, keep focusing on how you *feel* about the different thoughts that pass through your mind in words.

Exercises for Staying Focused on Your Feelings

These are exercises to help you learn to focus on your feelings when you are primarily verbal or visual. You will not need to use these during your sessions once you have developed skill with the Third Element. These exercises will help you to develop that skill, then you won't need them.

If you are primarily verbal:

- Close your eyes.
- Begin slow, full, Circular Breathing.
- Scan through your feeling awareness and find the most prominent sensation in this moment.
- Now begin describing the feeling to yourself in words. I don't mean to analyze it, or figure out where it came from, or even label it in any way. Instead, just keep describing it to yourself, much the same as if you were a sports announcer describing everything that's happening.
- Describe in words what the feeling feels like.
- Describe it's exact location.
- Describe it's various qualities and features.
- Give a running commentary on the changes it goes through as you keep exploring it.

This is a far better use of your mind than talking to yourself about your problems!

If you are primarily visual:

- Close your eyes and go into your space.
- Begin slow, full, Circular Breathing.
- Scan through your feeling awareness and find the most prominent sensation in this moment.
- Use your internal visual sense to look at the feeling, just as though all of the tissues in your body were transparent, except for the tissues in the strongest feeling.
- See it's location.
- See it's texture.
- See what color it is.
- And watch the subtle changes it goes through.

Tips for Improving Your Skill With the Third Element

Whenever you feel something, take a moment to notice exactly *where* you feel it in your body and just focus in on it. Do this with emotions. Do this with hunger, tiredness, caffeine stimulation, and so on.

Go to movies that you know will activate your emotions strongly, and while your emotions are activated keep focusing on where you feel the emotion in your body. (Interestingly, this process works much better with movies in a theater than with shows on television, because of the different effect that the two different media have on the nervous system.)

When your Vivation Professional thinks you are ready, doing some Vivation sessions in warm and cold water will help you to develop greater awareness of your body.

Practice "taking your body apart." This means relaxing and moving awareness around in your body, feeling each part of your body in the smallest detail possible. Start with your left foot and "dissect" each toe and each bone, muscle and tendon in your foot before moving on up your leg and to all the other parts of your body. At first it will be easier to do this exercise fairly quickly, taking maybe fifteen or twenty minutes to do your entire body. With practice you'll get to where you can spend one hour, or even longer, doing it very, very thoroughly.

Studying yoga, tai chi, martial arts, and other physical meditations will improve your Awareness in Detail.

In general, check in with yourself as often as you can to see what you are feeling. Do this in your car, at work, while waiting in the dentist's office, wherever and whenever you can. Even put up signs here and there to remind yourself.

Spending time in nature, by yourself or with others (but without talking) will improve your skill with Awareness in Detail.

CHAPTER 7

The Fourth Element of Vivation

INTEGRATION INTO ECSTASY

Integration into Ecstasy is the skill of embracing your most activated feeling. This means relating positively to a feeling that in the past may have seemed uncomfortable. By *embracing* the feeling, I mean accepting it, making peace with it, receiving energy from it, enjoying it, seeing it as perfect. You already have some degree of ability to accept things as they are, even when they are not the way you would prefer them to be. In learning to use the Fourth Element, you simply refine that ability into a powerful skill.

Integration into Ecstasy is simple, and yet it's different from what people usually do. Even more than that, it's different from what people say they do. So, I'm going to present the paradoxical nature of the words available for teaching this skill.

If I talk about *enjoying* pain, the idea doesn't sound right. You and I agree completely about that. But I want to tell you that this is not because of the nature of pain, itself, but rather because the *word* "pain" has a built-in negative context. Pain is just energy. Enjoying energy sounds fine, so when you have physical or emotional pain, let it just be "energy," and do not label it as pain. Very often in Vivation, feelings that start off being "painful" are integrated completely and become a source of pleasure.

If I talk about *accepting* pain, that sounds more reasonable than enjoying it. But then it sounds like the pain continues to be just as unpleasant as before, and you simply go through life passively putting up with it. That is not what I mean at all.

Because both "accepting it" and "enjoying it" are misleading, we need the word *integration* to explain the result of Vivation. The experience of pain (emotional or physical) transforms completely when it *integrates* during Vivation.

The word "ecstasy" means experiencing the perfection of everything. *Ecstasy* is the natural state of the real you, beyond your mind and personality. Integration into Ecstasy means making the connection between your natural state of ecstasy and an experience that has been troubling you. The result is that you enjoy your life more and live in harmony with your life's purpose.

The *content*, or "reality" of an experience, cannot be unpleasant or bad. The content simply is the way it is. If you are holding reality in a negative context, then the content will *seem* bad to you. It won't look to you like your way of relating to it is making an OK thing seem bad. It will look to you like the thing itself really is bad. Suppose you put on brown-colored sunglasses, and forget that you have them on. Everything will look rather colorless and unattractive to you until it occurs to you that it might just be the glasses.

There's a saying you might have heard: "I felt sorry for myself because I had no shoes until I met a man who had no legs." The saying is about integration. Even though you might think you need shoes to be happy, a change of perspective shows you that all you need in order to be happy is your legs, whether you have shoes or not. So, what do people need in order to be happy? Legs? Well, no. Many people without legs are happy, too. Existence itself is all you need to be happy. As long as you exist you can be grateful for your existence, even if everything else is different from what you might prefer.

Contextual Reality

If anything seems bad or unpleasant, it's because you are viewing it through a negative context. The exact same thing, viewed through a positive context (which only means that you are accepting it as it is) can be seen as something to be grateful for—no matter how bad it seemed through the negative context. People often get very, very upset about things that somebody else would be very, very grateful for. An example is that you could become very upset because a restaurant isn't preparing your food the way you ordered it. But someone who had recently been starving in Somalia would be extremely grateful for that same meal over which you were so upset.

The opportunity for gratitude and happiness is always available, even when it doesn't seem like it would be. The ability to change perspectives so that what seemed bad becomes good is what the Fourth Element is all about.

Another familiar saying is: "Do you see the glass as half-empty or half-full?" Please observe that something is only half-empty compared to an imaginary standard. The exact same amount of water would make a different glass completely full, and yet another glass only one-quarter full. When you focus on the water in the half-full part of the glass, you are focusing on what actually exists. The water is real, the perceived "emptiness" is an illusion created by the mind. All you are doing in integration is embracing what is actually there, letting go of insisting that it "should" be more or better.

This change of context from demanding an illusion to embracing reality always improves your experience immediately and makes you more powerful, effective and creative. It works with absolutely everything that seems unpleasant—from grief to anger, from head colds to arthritis.

In Vivation this change of context is applied to the feelings in the body. This works far more efficiently than applying it mentally. Vivation is extremely efficient, and in a one-hour session you can experience many, many integrations. The integration in Vivation is deep and permanent. The combination of all Five Elements is what produces the result so efficiently and so *physically*.

Integration into Ecstasy is essential in both the activation and the integration of suppressed material. It's essential to the process of activation because the feeling cannot be perceived accurately if your perception is clouded by make-wrong. It's essential to the integration of suppressed material because the embracing of previously-made-wrong feelings is what eliminates internal conflict and brings all your energy back into unified consciousness. Integration into Ecstasy supports the other four Elements and also depends upon the other four Elements. It supports the other four because receptivity to pleasure improves your breathing, relaxation, awareness and willingness. It depends upon the other four because energy is essential to the consciousness of ecstasy.

Going Where No Feeling Has Gone Before

Integration into Ecstasy is not the skill of blissing out peacefully with no feeling activated (or pretending that no feeling is activated). It is the skill of taking a feeling further into your sphere of enjoyment than you have before. Not all feelings that come up during Vivation are unpleasant. When the strongest feeling in your body is perceived to be unpleasant, Integration into Ecstasy is the skill of reducing your resistance to it, thus allowing it to become at least a little bit less unpleasant. When the strongest feeling in your body is perceived to be pleasant, you still have an apparent limit to how much you are able to enjoy it. (If you were able to enjoy any feeling infinitely, you would already be fully enlightened, consciously one with the Creator and the Creation, already perfect at Viving, and with no need for further instruction.)

When the strongest feeling in the body is perceived to be pleasant, the skill of Integration into Ecstasy is reducing even further your resistance to the pleasure, taking even more pleasure from it than you previously have done. Developing skill with Integration into Ecstasy results in taking in more and more of the good that life has to offer.

Learning to Use The Fourth Element

You already have enough skill with Integration into Ecstasy to achieve excellent, life-changing results in your Vivation session. Everything you do to increase your skill with Integration into Ecstasy will make your sessions even richer and more rewarding.

Different individuals have very different personal styles in how they apply the Fourth Element. Some people do it more by giving love to the feeling, some more by accepting the feeling, others more by being fascinated by the feeling, with infinite variations. You will develop your own individual style and your style will evolve as you gain experience with Vivation.

All you need is *any* way of relating to something you don't like that enables you to like it a little bit more. Once you have that, then you can simply broaden that skill to include more and more of your experiences.

For example, there may have been times that someone came into your life that you didn't like but had to accept because they were in-laws or co-workers or something. Eventually you may have even grown to like some of these people. If you can discover how you, within yourself, changed your perspective to see them as more acceptable, then you can cultivate that ability and use it to integrate all your feelings.

The Fourth Element is never about telling yourself that something is better than it actually is, and it is never about hoping that something will become better in the future. Everything that exists is how you want it to be to some extent. The Fourth Element is simply focusing on how good something is, rather than on how bad it is, similar to focusing on the half-full part of the glass.

Using Vivation over a period of time will greatly increase your ability to apply Integration into Ecstasy. Each integration will make your next integration easier. People having their first Vivation session vary widely in the skill they already have with Integration into Ecstasy. You, personally, might already be very skillful at embracing life experiences. Or you might be habitually critical of people, things and experiences you don't like. Either way, you can learn to embrace everything exactly as it is. This is always profoundly to your advantage.

Keep It Simple

In learning Integration into Ecstasy, keep it simple! Some people do best starting with a comparatively philosophical approach to Integration into Ecstasy. That's fine. I'll explain how to do that. But listen: Learn it intellectually but don't keep it intellectual! Intellectual approaches to the Fourth Element interfere with the Third Element.

Within your first few Vivation sessions you want to be able to let go of your mind completely and still have the Fourth Element work consistently.

Philosophy either works for you on an energy level or it doesn't work at all. If something philosophical helps you to integrate an unpleasant feeling, then it is working for you on an energy level. This is true even if the philosophical point is stated in words. Words are simply mental symbols for experiences. If you use words to learn how to make an integrative connection with a feeling, then learn to drop the words and still make the same connection.

Different statements of how to have a positive relationship to something are called Fourth Element Techniques. Each of these represents an energy connection you make within yourself. Even though these are stated in words, do not try to apply them during your session by saying them to yourself in words. Instead learn to make the energy connection by practicing (as explained here) and then keep making the connection throughout your session.

For example, if you enjoy eating an apple, you don't need to say to yourself, "Enjoy this" or anything else. You just enjoy it. When you enjoy something, you relate to it in a particular positive way. You could eat the same apple and not enjoy it, by relating to it differently, for instance by comparing it to a better apple, or by wishing you were eating chocolate instead. Enjoyment is a skill. Practice enjoying, with concentration and focus, and you will increase your *ability* to enjoy. Then you can apply that skill to a broader range of experiences. You can use your heightened skill of enjoyment to integrate whatever feelings come up during your Vivation session.

You make a somewhat different energy connection if you focus on just accepting your experience of the present moment without labeling it as either good or bad. This will integrate anything that ever comes up just as well as enjoying it will.

Yet another integrative energy connection is made by being grateful that what you are experiencing is not worse than it is. Obviously, no matter how bad anything is, you can always be grateful that it's not worse, so you can use this energy connection to integrate absolutely anything.

There are infinitely many ways to make the integrative energy connection. In this chapter you'll find a list of one hundred of these. Each one takes a different route to arrive at the same destination, an energy connection between your inner ecstasy and something you've been making wrong. Each one can give you the power to integrate everything in your life that you have ever made wrong and suppressed.

Just because I list a hundred different ways to learn the Fourth Element doesn't mean you have to learn all hundred! I'm presenting a large variety to make sure that everybody can find several to which they can relate. Also, this list is obviously incomplete. You may have some other way of applying the Fourth Element that works best for you but is not on this list.

Read through the entire list. You will probably find that some of them remind you of things you have experienced before in your life. And you may find that some of them seem wrong or incomprehensible. Simply ignore the ones you don't like and take note of the ones you do like. Mark the ones you do like with a pencil, if you don't mind writing in books.

Now go back through the ones you have marked and choose your favorite one. Practice doing this one with many different kinds of things that you don't like. Bring into your mind a person whom you don't like, and apply the technique to your experience of that person. Bring to mind a task you don't enjoy and apply it to that task. Find an uncomfortable emotion or physical sensation and apply the technique to that. Practice this until you can do it quickly and easily without much thought.

Make this energy connection at the beginning of your Vivation session and maintain it and strengthen it as your session progresses. Your Vivation Professional will help you do this.

It is all right to have more than one Fourth Element technique that you use regularly. However, you do not want to use your mind to choose between them during your Vivation session. You want the integrative energy connection to be continuous. Be patient with yourself in developing this continuity.

FOURTH ELEMENT TECHNIQUES
or
100 Ways to Have A Positive Relationship to Anything

1. Enjoy it unconditionally.

2. Just accept it as it is without labeling it either good or bad.

3. Be grateful it's not worse.

4. Focus on your gratitude for your existence and expand that gratitude to include the experience you're having now.

5. Surrender to the fact that it is the way it is whether you like it or not.

6. Compare it only to itself.

7. Cultivate a sense of fascination with it - notice that it's at least interesting.

8. Expand your compassion for all people who experience similar things.

9. Be open to it making a contribution to you somehow.

10. Extend unconditional love to all parts of your experience.

11. Turn your whole experience over to God.

12. Appreciate that it is exactly the way it is for only this one moment in all of eternity.

13. Enjoy it quick, before it integrates.

14. Notice how close you are to integrating it.

15. Acknowledge that it's obviously the way some part of you wants it to be.

16. Appreciate that it helps you get to know yourself better.

17. Acknowledge that it would be OK to lighten up about it.

18. Imagine what it would be like for it to be exactly as it is but for you to feel OK about it.

19. Notice the extent to which you already do feel OK about it.

20. Since you know you'll make peace with it eventually, decide to make peace with it now.

21. Enthusiastically exaggerate your feeling.

22. You know you like intense experiences, so enjoy it because *at least it's intense*!

23. Be comfortable with its familiarity.

24. Be grateful that the right thing is activated.

25. Claim your good from it.

26. Enjoy the newness of it.

27. Be grateful for your ability to feel.

28. Know that by feeling it you are healing it.

29. Notice that, in a certain way, what you are experiencing is funny.

30. Honor it as a teacher.

31. Stay open-minded about it.

32. Knowing that beyond the conditioning of your mind, the real you is ecstatic about it, choose to have your conscious mind be ecstatic as well.

33. Laugh at the absurdity of making anything wrong.

34. Notice that, considering what you did to make it this way, it didn't turn out as badly as it might have.

35. Acknowledge the benefit you are getting from it now.

36. Notice how it strengthens your relationship with God.

37. Notice how it strengthens your character.

38. Notice how it strengthens your determination.

39. Be grateful for what a good story it will allow you to tell later on!

40. Let the curtain close on your drama.

41. Allow the Holy Spirit to enter your body and heal all parts of you.

42. Even if it doesn't seem pleasurable, open up to it as though it were pleasurable.

43. Feel the tingle of aliveness within the pattern of energy.

44. Experience every sensation as an instrument of God's love.

45. Notice that it's a miracle that this moment exists at all and bliss out on the miracle of its existence.

46. Receive the energy from this pattern of energy.

47. Trust that you are strong enough to handle even the worst of it.

48. Realize that it's not as bad as your worst thoughts about it.

49. Command it to be the way it already is.

50. Relax your mind.

51. Be enthusiastic about integrating it.

52. Praise it unconditionally.

53. Pretend that it is easy to integrate.

54. Be very gentle, patient and caring with yourself in the presence of the feelings.

55. Know that God's love for you is unconditional.

56. Be grateful that it's coming up at such an appropriate time.

57. Just say "yes" to the feeling.

58. Love the part of you that's activated.

59. Notice that the feelings in your body can't be weirder than you are.

60. Let the pleasurable feelings of strength and vigor that are already present in your body help you to integrate it.

61. Experience every sensation as white light or healing energy.

62. Let your love of Vivation expand to include everything that comes up in your session.

63. Acknowledge that at least the honesty with which you feel the feelings feels good.

64. Be grateful that it gives you something to Vive into.

65. Let the feeling take you on an adventure.

66. Acknowledge that you've struggled with it long enough, and just let go.

67. Notice that the Creator of the Universe obviously thinks it's supposed to be exactly like this right now.

68. Let it be just a pattern of energy.

69. Acknowledge that, as part of the perfect Universe, you must be perfect.

70. Experience its energy as God's own energy.

71. Welcome this opportunity to let go of ego.

72. Appreciate how it rebalances your energy.

73. Be grateful that you know how to Vive!

74. Notice that the same God who gave you life and every wonderful thing you've ever experienced is in charge of this also.

75. Acknowledge your feeling in this moment as your most direct connection to the Divine.

76. Be grateful that at least you're a classy enough snob to know a poor quality experience when you're having one!

77. Find the presence of God within the feeling.

78. Appreciate its unique beauty.

79. Be grateful that this experience lets you know you're alive.

80. Be grateful that you have such a marvelous excuse for your negativity.

81. Trust your body.

82. Acknowledge that being honest with these feelings puts you on the right track for getting what you want.

83. Trust that everything is evolving perfectly.

84. Trust that, since other people have made it through this, you can, too.

85. Acknowledge that the stuff that's bothering you is not what really matters the most in life anyway.

86. Be grateful for how this experience educates you.

87. Welcome the challenge of integrating it.

88. Acknowledge that you are doing the right thing to integrate it.

89. Trust in the inevitability of integration.

90. Experience that you love yourself enough to stay with it until it integrates.

91. Just choose love.

92. Acknowledge that judging it negatively is costing you too high a price.

93. Surrender to the fact that you just can't win a war against your own feelings.

94. Love the energy in your body unconditionally.

95. Laugh at your mind's reaction to it.

96. Be grateful that the part of your body where you feel this activation exists at all.

97. Try making it worse instead of better.

98. Be grateful that what's happening now is leading up to your next wonderful experience.

99. Make peace with everything.

100. Enjoy it because this is the only life you have.

Even if you find these hundred ways helpful in the beginning, you won't always need them. With practice you will learn to maintain the integrative energy connection without even having to think about it.

You can also do the Fourth Element physically from the very beginning. You simply focus on receiving the energy from the pattern of energy. You don't have to have any idea at all what the feeling is about or any idea what could possibly be good about it. You don't need any positive context in your mind at all.

Here is one more extremely important point about applying the Fourth Element. Do not fall into the trap of *trying hard* to integrate something. If your Fourth Element technique doesn't work at all, don't worry about it.

Here is one more extremely important point about applying the Fourth Element. Do not fall into the trap of *trying hard* to integrate something. If your Fourth Element technique doesn't work at all, don't worry about it. Be patient and just keep focusing on the feeling, and applying all the other skills of Vivation. The feeling will definitely integrate, if you just keep focusing on it, because you'll get used to the feeling and run out of desire to continue resisting it. If you just continue your session, Integration into Ecstasy will happen automatically within a short time. This will occur in less time if you don't struggle to find some way to integrate the feeling. But even if you do struggle to integrate it, integration will still happen before long. I reiterate: Integration is inevitable if you just keep Viving.

Developing More Skill With Integration Into Ecstasy

Every morning choose a Fourth Element technique and sit and practice it for a few minutes. Then throughout the day remind yourself of it and apply it to everything that you experience. It can be an excellent idea to write reminders of the technique on signs or even on the back of your hand to remind you.

Anything that gives you pleasure or increases your enjoyment of life will support you in developing skill with the Fourth Element. Contrary to what you may have been taught elsewhere, PLEASURE IS GOOD FOR YOU! This is particularly true if you focus on taking in as much pleasure as you possibly can, even more pleasure than seems initially to be available from the kind of experience you're having.

Anything that helps you to develop greater mental flexibility will help. Some examples: Traveling in foreign countries will help you to see things from different points of view. Studying comparative religion or different philosophies can be very helpful. Also, challenging yourself by going to concerts of different kinds of music than you usually listen to, or political rallies of the parties you don't like. Staying out of a rut will help you.

Laughter will improve your skill with the Fourth Element. The more you laugh, the better. Go to comedy clubs. Watch silly movies. Hang out with droll friends. Also, as an exercise: just laugh, whether or not you can think of anything funny, even if you have to fake it at first. (Repeat after me: Ha! Ha! Ha! Ha! Ha!) This is an excellent exercise to do for five minutes or more, first thing when you wake up in the morning, either by yourself, or in a group.

Every kind of spiritual experience will make you better at Integration into Ecstasy. For some people, going to church will accomplish this, and for others, meditation or chanting. Perhaps you like making shrines around your house. Or putting up pictures of Jesus or your guru.

Playing with children or pets will help you to not take life so seriously and will help you develop skill with the Fourth Element.

No matter how much or how little you have enjoyed your life in the past, you can enjoy your life a whole lot more. Dedicate yourself to developing The Skill of Happiness.

CHAPTER 8

The Fifth Element of Vivation

DO WHATEVER YOU DO—WILLINGNESS IS ENOUGH

Vivation provides you with an infinite margin for error. There isn't any way to do Vivation wrong. You will always get excellent results, provided you have the willingness to embrace the honest experience of your feelings. You don't have to breathe right. You don't have to relax completely. You don't have to be perfectly attuned to the feeling. You don't have to find anything positive about anything. All Five Elements are skills, and the better you apply the skills, the better results you will get. However, the only thing you really must have in order to get excellent results is *willingness*.

Almost every activity in the world is different from Vivation. With almost everything else, there exists some right way to do it. There's a right way to do your taxes. There's a right way to build a house. There might even be a right way to eat. But there is no such thing as a right way to Vive.

That's because Vivation is a paradoxical skill. When you integrate something, what you are actually doing is allowing something to be the way it is. That's not nothing! Actually it's a lot! Nearly everybody goes through life struggling against many things being the way they are. In Vivation you let go of that struggle. Vivation is a skill that can fascinate you for a lifetime. You can get better and better at it forever. But it is still a paradox because instead of doing something, you are ceasing to do something. You are ceasing to suppress your feelings, and you are ceasing to resist life.

The essential skill of the Fifth Element is cultivating your willingness to experience reality fully. I know you might say, Yes, definitely! Of course I'm willing to experience reality fully!" But this willingness is not something you can simply declare. Moment by moment, feeling by feeling, breath by breath, your willingness is put to the test. Your willingness to experience reality fully must be cultivated, because reality includes a lot of suffering. All Five Elements are skills and the Fifth Element is the central skill from which all of the others spring.

An essential part of willingness to experience reality fully is letting go of all perceived preconditions for doing so. Let go of wanting things to get better first, before you experience them fully. Let go of thinking you need to do something right first, before you can experience reality fully. Let go of thinking that anything at all needs to happen first. Embrace reality as it is right now, before anything changes in any way.

The present moment is the way it is, and in Vivation you embrace the perfection of that. Part of what exists in the present moment is what you are *doing* in the present moment. Embracing the perfection of reality means embracing the perfection of what you are doing right now. For example, suppose you are Viving and you really just aren't getting the breathing right, you're controlling the exhale or something. That is perfect just like everything else about the present moment is perfect. Integration is available in this moment, regardless of how you're breathing. If you have the willingness to embrace reality, including your "wrong" breathing, you will have integration. If you "properly" relax the exhale, but you don't have willingness to embrace reality, you will not have integration.

The Fifth Element is stated in a different way than the other four Elements. The first four Elements are stated in momentary time. (Momentary time is the context in which the present moment is all that is considered to be real.) The Fifth Element is the only one that is stated in linear time. (Linear time is the context in which one moment comes after another, the future and past are considered real, and you are doing, rather than simply experiencing.) This is because the first four Elements are conditions you maintain in the present moment. The Fifth Element addresses what you have to do next in order to achieve integration. *Do whatever you actually do.* You don't have to do any particular thing in order to have integration. If you have the willingness to integrate, then it doesn't matter what you do. It's just not about doing. The results in Vivation do not come from what you should do, nor from how a session should go. The results come from *willingness*.

Here's an example that illustrates the Fifth Element. Sometimes someone asks me, "Jim, if I'm in a session and I get thirsty, if I drink some water am I suppressing the thirst?" The answer is, it's not about that. You can drink the water and suppress the thirst, or drink the water and integrate the thirst, or not drink the water and suppress the thirst, or not drink the water and integrate the thirst. Whatever you actually do is the right thing for you to do. Whether you integrate the thirst or not is determined by your willingness or lack of willingness, not by anything that you do or don't do.

You can do all the other Elements much more skillfully when you know they are not preconditions of integration. For example, if you say to yourself, "If only I could just tune this feeling in a little better, I could integrate it," that interferes with giving the present moment your full attention. There is tremendous relief and freedom in realizing that if you are willing to integrate, you will, and if you're not willing, you won't! What you get is your desired result!

This principle of the Fifth Element can be illustrated by a story my father used to tell about one of his co-workers. Every day this guy would open up his lunch box and complain bitterly about his lunch. He'd open his lunch box and say, "Spam sandwich again! I can't stand this any more! Every day the same darned thing!" After hearing this day after day, my father finally asked him, "Well, why don't you ask your wife to make you something different for lunch?" The man replied, "It's got nothing to do with my wife! I always make my own darn lunch!"

The Fifth Element is simply remaining conscious of the fact that you are the one who is creating your experience. To think something has to happen first before you can achieve integration is to make yourself a victim.

Trying to do Vivation right is not part of doing it skillfully. However, you will get excellent results even when you are trying to do it right, provided you have willingness.

You never need to be more willing than you actually are. You don't have to become willing first before you integrate. If you are willing to be willing, that is already enough willingness.

All Five Elements work together. You can do all the Elements more skillfully when you know that your results come from your willingness and not from achieving mechanical perfection with the technique. Trying to do it right carries with it an implied make-wrong, that there is an imaginary standard to compare yourself to in how you do this. Vivation is embracing consciously the present moment. In every moment you are doing something, and your doing is certainly one of the most important things you experience in any moment. It is impossible to embrace your doing without the Fifth Element. Vivation is utterly impossible without it.

Similarly, all the other Elements are essential to your skillful use of the Fifth Element. Circular Breathing facilitates the Fifth Element because the energy flow itself suggests universal perfection. Complete Relaxation improves your skill with the Fifth Element because as you relax you let go. Awareness in Detail helps you apply the Fifth Element by showing you the most important reality you must be willing to embrace. And Integration into Ecstasy helps you develop skill with the Fifth Element because you are embracing all of your experience, including what you are doing in the present moment.

Vivation is a bit like dancing. When you learn a new dance, you try to do the steps right, but you don't want to be mechanical on the dance floor, you want to let go and just dance. The Fifth Element is letting go and just Viving.

Vivation is a little like making love. With experience you get better at love-making and with experience you get better at Viving. In both love-making and Vivation, trying to do it right is not the best thing to focus your attention on. Willingness is enough!

When you are first learning Vivation, Vivation is a technique. Once you gain some experience with it, you begin to realize that it isn't really a technique after all. Embracing reality is the essence of Vivation, and embracing reality is not technique. You don't embrace reality in order to accomplish something, you embrace it because it is real, and self-delusion has ceased to be an attractive option.

Cultivating More Skill With The Fifth Element

Allowing yourself to be more spontaneous in conversation will help you with the Fifth Element. The more you think you need to be careful what you say, the less you'll see that you can't violate universal perfection.

Dancing will help you develop the Fifth Element, and the more free-form the dance, the better.

All sorts of courageous risk-taking will help you to develop the skills and attitudes that support the Fifth Element.

Being in nature, looking at the ocean, watching sunrises and sunsets, gazing at the night sky all help with the Fifth Element because they remind you that the universe continues to take care of itself perfectly without your having to do anything right.

Spending time with babies helps you develop skill with the Fifth Element, because they live on willingness alone until their technical and verbal skills develop.

Telling the truth helps the Fifth Element. One of many disadvantages of lying is that it takes you further away from your willingness to experience the fullness of reality and takes you further away from trusting the Universe. Lying also requires being careful.

Anything you do to help alleviate the suffering of others will improve your skill with the Fifth Element, because the willingness to be real with anyone's suffering is the same as willingness to be real with your own.

Don't worry about doing Vivation right. Just keep Viving!

CHAPTER 9

THE THREE POINTS TO REMEMBER

The Three Points to Remember make Vivation extremely simple to do. I consider The Three Points to Remember the most important breakthrough in Vivation methodology since I invented Vivation in 1979. They make the process much easier to teach and far more powerful. Everyone has better sessions when they use them.

Before I developed The Three Points to Remember, the Viver had to continuously monitor all Five Elements. Obviously that works perfectly, but now The Three Points to Remember make Vivation work even better!

The first thing you need to understand about this is that The Five Elements and The Three Points to Remember are totally different kinds of things. As you have seen, each of The Five Elements represents a substantial body of knowledge. The Three Points to Remember, in contrast, are not bodies of knowledge at all, but simple things you do on the inside during your session. Used well, *each one* of The Three Points to Remember maintains *all five* Elements.

In order to Vive with The Three Points to Remember, you must be able to use all three. But during a session, you can use them one at a time. Do each Point with your fullest possible concentration. After a while, you may find that your ability to concentrate on one Point starts to fade. That is because of the nature of concentration, not because of the nature of you or The Three Points to Remember. When that happens, just shift to another of The Three Points, and do that with your fullest possible concentration. You can rotate through them, doing each one for a little while, until you naturally move on to the next. You can also use any combination of two at a time or all three at once. Using The Three Points to Remember makes Vivation a more spontaneous dance of consciousness than ever!

Please understand that The Five Elements, in contrast, do not work if you try to apply them one at a time. You must maintain all Five Elements simultaneously in order to have integration. The great thing about The Three Points to Remember is you don't have to think about all Five Elements in order to maintain them all simultaneously. It happens automatically as a result of concentrating on any one of The Three Points to Remember.

To learn to use The Three Points to Remember (or anything else in this book) you will need to go to a Vivation Professional and get some Vivation sessions. I sincerely doubt that even the most brilliant, tuned-in person in the world can learn Vivation from a book, even if the book is the most brilliant book in the world. Vivation is like flying an airplane or playing the violin. You need to get some lessons from a teacher.

Vivation is thirteen years older than The Three Points to Remember—there are many excellent Vivation Professionals who have never been trained in how to use The Three Points. Any Vivation Professional can teach you how to Vive, and you will get great sessions and change your life as a result. Feel free to get sessions from any Vivation Professional you want. But you might have the experience of phoning up a Vivation Professional and asking about The Three Points to Remember and getting a response of either, "I don't know what you are talking about," or, "I don't do it that way."

The Three Points to Remember cannot be understood from their names alone, any more than the Five Elements can be. They must be defined, demonstrated, tried and refined. Vivation Professionals who have been trained in this system can lead you through a series of experiential exercises to make sure you learn how to do what is described in this chapter. What I shall do is give you an introduction to each one of The Three Points to Remember and explain how this system works.

These are The Three Points to Remember:

1. Explore the subtle changes.
2. Inhale through the strongest feeling.
3. Enjoy this moment as much as you can.

1) Explore the Subtle Changes

Every perception you ever have of anything is constantly changing in subtle ways. This is not just because everything is actually changing—some things are changing so subtly or so slowly that you couldn't possibly perceive the change. But even if you just sit by yourself in a brightly lit room and stare at the wall, your actual perception of the wall will change in subtle ways that you can readily experience. This is because the normal nervous system is alive with chaos. In a way, you can explore the subtle changes with any of your senses, internal or external. But, of course, what I am talking about is exploring the subtle changes within whatever feeling in your body is strongest in the present moment.

The way to use "Explore the Subtle Changes" is to find the strongest feeling in your body, give it your fullest attention, and tune it in well enough to notice the subtle changes that happen in it from moment to moment. Often each strongest feeling will last for only a short time before some other feeling becomes the strongest. When that happens, shift immediately from the old strongest feeling to the new one. Just follow the energy around your body with your consciousness. Other times, the same feeling will last for a relatively long time. Then you stay focused on it and continue following the subtle changes that happen within that feeling.

A major benefit of exploring the subtle changes during Vivation is that it keeps you in present time. It is impossible to focus on the subtle changes without being absolutely present. In fact, exploring the subtle changes can even be an excellent definition of the phrase "Be here now."

Exploring the subtle changes also helps you with Circular Breathing. When you are focused on the subtle changes, your breathing automatically adjusts itself properly to stay in sync with the strongest feeling in your body, which is what you always want.

Exploring the subtle changes helps you relax by bringing receptive, rather than controlling, consciousness to the muscles that are tense. Tension is a result of control. Exploring the subtle changes automatically puts you in a mode of receptivity that reduces control.

"Explore the Subtle Changes" helps you stay in the Third Element, because in order to integrate a feeling you have to be aware of it in sufficient detail. If you are focusing on the subtle changes that happen within the feeling from moment to moment, that is always sufficient detail for integration.

Another benefit of exploring the subtle changes is that it "uses up" the restless, searching part of your mind. It allows you to get your mind out of your way and simply experience the energy without labels or words.

Exploring the subtle changes shows you that your most activated feeling is not stuck. Whenever people are making anything wrong, part of them thinks the thing is stuck. That's an essential quality of make-wrong. Thus exploring the subtle changes is a very practical way to eliminate both suppression and make-wrong.

Yet another benefit of exploring the subtle changes is that it helps you to feel that your body is not solid matter, but rather a body of energy. This is an essential step in getting to know your own individual spirit. It is the essence of integration.

Exploring the subtle changes also makes your connection to God more conscious. This moment has come about because of an unbroken chain of cause and effect that goes back to the beginning of time. Your body and everything else that exists is the result of subtle changes that have been happening from moment to moment since the very beginning. Those same subtle changes that have created everything are continuing even now. When you focus on the subtle changes that happen from moment to moment in your feelings, you are focusing on the Creative Power of God at work inside your own body. This is the most satisfying experience there is.

Exploring the subtle changes increases the Fifth Element in two ways. It increases willingness to experience feelings honestly by giving a direct experience that doing so is pleasurable. It reduces thinking that you need to do something right by showing you that everything is evolving perfectly without your having to do anything better or differently than you already are.

2) Inhale Through The Strongest Feeling

Focus on the part of your body where the feeling is strongest at the moment, and pull each inhale into your body through that place. Obviously you physically breathe in through your nose or mouth, but with your consciousness take the breath in through the part of your body where the feeling is strongest. You can just pretend you have a nose there, if that helps. It's as though, just because you have the feeling there, that part of your body becomes permeable to air. As the feelings move around in your body, change where you pull the breath in as well.

I want to explain what I don't mean. I do not mean that you pull the breath in through your nose or mouth and then send the energy to the part of your body where the feeling is strongest. Doing that will not produce the same result and will not work as a Point to Remember. The air actually enters your body through the top of your head, or your stomach ache, or your knee, or whatever. If this doesn't quite make sense to you, that's fine. You won't really be able to use this just by reading about it anyway, you need to be led through experiential exercises by a Vivation Professional in order to use The Three Points to Remember.

Inhaling through the strongest feeling makes it much easier to coordinate the Circular Breathing with the feeling on which you are focusing.

Inhaling through the strongest feeling gives very strong support to the Second Element, because it is the very essence of massaging yourself from the inside. If you have a tense muscle, just pull the breath in through the muscle for a while, and it will relax.

If you inhale through the strongest feeling, the feeling itself will become more vivid, so doing so supports the Third Element.

Inhaling through the strongest feeling greatly assists in applying the Fourth Element. As you receive the inhale through the feeling you receive whatever good that feeling has to offer you.

Inhaling through the strongest feeling increases your application of the Fifth Element because doing so is an expression of your willingness. Inhaling through the feeling shows that you are willing to experience the feeling honestly. Also with each inhale you receive benefit from a feeling that you were previously resisting, thus proving, on a feeling level, that you don't have to do anything right in order to receive something good.

"Inhale Through the Strongest Feeling" works because air is more than molecules. The physical molecules of air come in through your nose or mouth no matter where you pretend to pull it in. But air is also energy, and you really do pull in energy through (and from) your heart or your toe or wherever you focus. Thus, inhaling through the strongest feeling increases your perception of your body as an energy system, which is integrative in its own right.

3) Enjoy This Moment As Much As You Can

"Enjoy This Moment as Much as You Can" means you focus on the present moment and notice that it is pleasurable to some extent. Even if it is a particularly unpleasant moment, it still is not *infinitely* unpleasant. Even the worst moment is at least one per cent pleasurable, because existence itself is fundamentally pleasurable. When you have an experience that is only one per cent pleasurable, it is even more important to connect with that one per cent.

Focus on the pleasure you can find in the present moment and *try your hardest* to enjoy this moment infinitely. It doesn't matter at all whether you get a little pleasure or a lot from the present moment. What matters is that you absorb whatever pleasure is there to your maximum capacity. "Enjoy This Moment as Much as You Can" is not the same thing as the Fourth Element. In order to make this work as a Point to Remember, you must make the extra "effort" to take every last drop of pleasure from the moment.

"Enjoy This Moment as Much as You Can" improves your Circular Breathing because as you take each inhale you naturally draw the feeling into your loving awareness. Also you will make exactly the right adjustments to the breathing, because the right adjustments are exactly the ones that maximize your enjoyment of the feeling.

"Enjoy This Moment as Much as You Can" relaxes you by directly reducing your struggle.

"Enjoy This Moment as Much as You Can" gives particularly strong support to the Third Element. If you intentionally take the maximum amount of pleasure that you possibly can from the present moment, then whatever is preventing you from enjoying the present moment infinitely will stand out in sharp contrast. Also, whenever you focus on enjoying anything you naturally focus on experiencing its details more vividly.

This Point obviously supports the Fourth Element by making you more receptive to the good side of whatever you are focusing on.

"Enjoy This Moment as Much as You Can" increases your application of the Fifth Element both by expressing and increasing your willingness. If you are willing to enjoy the feeling you've been making wrong, that is clearly the exact willingness the Fifth Element is about. It also gives you the experience that even with everything you have ever done "wrong," your life is still excellent.

Learning to Use The Three Points to Remember

Once you have been led through the experiential exercises for learning The Three Points to Remember, you can begin using The Three Points during your sessions. You still have to stay in all Five Elements in order to get results. For example when focusing on "Explore the Subtle Changes," you still have to keep your breathing Circular. Another example is that you have to keep relaxing or else when you enjoy this moment as much as you can, you might get up and start dancing (which would be fun, but would not maximize your integration of suppressed feelings).

Even with using The Three Points to Remember, it is still absolutely true that anything you do to improve your skill with any of The Five Elements will help you to produce better results for yourself. At the same time, no matter how deeply you develop your understanding of The Five Elements, I still suggest using The Three Points to

Remember as what you *actually do* during your session. The Three Points to Remember can make your sessions much more effective by allowing you to focus on doing only one thing at a time. Using The Three Points to Remember has made a tremendous difference in my own sessions.

I crafted The Three Points to Remember especially to support the Third Element, which is the Element the vast majority of people need the most help with, especially when they are new to Vivation. This is one reason why new clients benefit enormously from learning The Three Points to Remember from the very beginning. My experience has also been that even very experienced Vivers, who already consistently produce excellent results, experience immediate and lasting improvement in the quality of their sessions when they begin using the Three Points to Remember.

To use this system, you must use all Three Points to Remember. Make sure you develop good skill with each one. If you find that you are not able to do any one of the Three Points to Remember skillfully, then continue to use the Five Elements for your sessions.

Once you have learned to use The Three Points well, just dance through them, staying with each one for the time that you can do so with complete concentration. Integrations will happen during each phase, while you are focusing on each of the three.

In this way, changing among The Three Points to Remember every little while, you are able to stay very present in your session, maintain all Five Elements without having to think about them, and have a richly satisfying experience in which you integrate many feelings.

CHAPTER 10

YOUR PERSONAL VIVATION PROGRAM

You owe it to yourself to get a Vivation session, to experience for yourself The Skill of Happiness! Reading this book and never getting a session would be like reading about chocolate and never tasting any.

You are ready to start, right now. Not one thing needs to change first in you or in your life before you get started. If your mind says to you, "You're not ready yet," that is the same part of your mind that suppresses your feelings and tells you that you are limited in other ways, too. Put that part of your mind in its place.

The only way you can have the experience of Vivation is by learning from a Vivation Professional. Trying to learn Vivation without getting any sessions from a Vivation Professional is like trying to learn to play the violin without getting any instruction. If you simply put the bow to the strings, you will get some sound, some result, but probably not the result you are hoping for. You also cannot learn Vivation from people who teach other kinds of breathing techniques. That would be like trying to learn how to play the violin by going to a swimming instructor.

Your first Vivation session will be an amazing experience. You will permanently resolve emotions that have been causing you problems. You will feel your own individual spirit vividly. And you will start on your path of mastering the Vivation process.

This chapter tells you how to get started and what to expect your process of learning Vivation to be like. I explain how to customize your use of Vivation to suit your individual needs and how to progress toward mastery of the process.

How to Get Started

The first step is to contact Associated Vivation Professionals. Associated Vivation Professionals (AVP) is a worldwide professional organization of people dedicating their lives to making Vivation available to the public. AVP will provide you a list of Vivation Professionals in your area, let you know about upcoming seminars, and provide you with other literature and services that you will find helpful. Here is where to contact AVP:

Associated Vivation Professionals
PO Box 2595
Minneapolis, MN 55402
From the United States or Canada, phone TOLL FREE:
1-800-829-2625
From outside the USA and Canada, phone:
001-612-377-VIVE

You have a variety of options for how to get started with Vivation. You can get a private session. You can go to an introductory seminar, possibly just one evening, which will provide you with information and which may or may not contain an actual Vivation session. You can take a one-day or weekend seminar, which will provide substantial instruction and one or more full Vivation sessions. In some areas you will be able to join an ongoing group which meets weekly or monthly for an extended period of time—this option provides the significant benefit of community, about which I have more to say later. You can also take a Vivation Professional Training, which is suitable for beginners as well as for people who are studying to become Vivation Professionals. Seminars and Trainings are led regularly throughout the world by Vivation Professionals of local, national and international prominence. If you learn Vivation initially from someone who lives outside your area, you will still want to develop an ongoing professional relationship with a Vivation Professional near you.

Regardless of how you decide to get started, your first step will be learning the internal skill of integrating emotions. Your Vivation Professional will teach this to you by leading you through a series of experiential exercises. If you start with a private session you will have the benefit of complete privacy, the undivided attention of your Vivation Professional, and a presentation individually tailored to suit you personally. If you start with a group you will have the benefit of other participants' questions and experiences, which is a substantial benefit.

Your Vivation Professional provides two different main categories of service: education and facilitation. Your Vivation Professional teaches you the skills of Vivation and continues helping you develop your skills in every session.

Your Vivation Professional also coaches you through your sessions. You will get vastly more from your sessions because of the coaching your Vivation Professional gives you, particularly in the beginning. The coach can see when you go out of any of The Five Elements and say or do things to support that Element. You will learn how to do this for yourself, as I explain later in this chapter. But having someone watch from the outside will enable you to go much further in your sessions, and get far more benefit.

For example, when you are Viving, you try to stay focused on the feelings in your body without going off into your mind too much. Even very skillful Vivers drift off into thoughts and images from time to time and have to pull themselves back to focus on their feelings. Even when you're skillful, it still takes you a little time to realize that you have gone out of your body. A Vivation Professional can recognize the very moment you go off into thoughts, by watching your eye movement under your closed eyelids, and then remind you to come back. This is just one example, related to the Third Element. Your Vivation Professional can recognize when you stray from any one of The Five Elements.

What Is A Vivation Professional?

A Vivation Professional is a person whose love of Vivation is so great that they feel they want to share Vivation with the world. Vivation Professionals dedicate themselves to constantly improving their own skills with Vivation. They continuously develop their ability to teach Vivation and to coach sessions. All Vivation Professionals are members of Associated Vivation Professionals. (The law requires being a member of AVP if you call yourself a Vivation Professional or offer Vivation to clients.)

Most Vivation Professionals have taken one or more Vivation Professional Trainings. Some have learned to be Vivation Professionals in other ways, for example by doing an apprenticeship with a Vivation Professional. All Vivation Professionals have extensive experience at using Vivation themselves.

Remember that Vivation is a self-applied skill and is not therapy for any condition. You produce all of your own results in Vivation. The result Vivation produces is integration of feelings and not anything else. Most Vivation Professionals are not psychotherapists or physicians, although some are. Even if you go to a Vivation Professional who is a psychotherapist or physician, the Vivation sessions you receive from them do not constitute psychotherapy or medical treatment.

How to Choose Your Vivation Professional

Once you have a list of Vivation Professionals, I suggest phoning them to ask them about their services, fees, availability, and so on.

You want to find a Vivation Professional who is right for you. It would not be a true statement to say that some Vivation Professionals are better than other Vivation Professionals. What is true is that some Vivation Professionals are better for some clients and other Vivation Professionals are better for other clients.

I definitely recommend that you not choose your Vivation Professional on the basis of price. Fees charged by Vivation Professionals vary enormously. The highest priced Vivation Professionals might charge as much as five times the fees charged by the lowest priced Vivation Professionals. A high-priced Vivation Professional might help you learn to do the process by yourself faster, and so might turn out to be less expensive in the long run than a low-priced Vivation Professional. However, do not assume that paying a higher fee will necessarily get you a better Vivation Professional. You might get the best results with the least expensive Vivation Professional! The price is simply irrelevant. Choose your Vivation Professional on the basis of who you most want to work with.

Sometimes Vivation Professionals who charge relatively high fees for private sessions also offer programs that are much less expensive and nearly as good. For example, many Vivation Professionals give four people at once a "semi-private" session, charging each client approximately one-fourth of the private session price. If you want to work with a relatively high-priced Vivation Professional, and feel that you cannot afford his or her fees, don't give up. Just tell your chosen Vivation Professional that you would like to know if there are other options you can afford.

The Economy of Vivation

Vivation with even the most costly Vivation Professionals in the world is not really very expensive when you consider the benefits. Doing Vivation is cheaper than not doing Vivation. The most expensive thing in the world is your own make-wrong, suppression and negativity. If you consider the money alone, Vivation will probably increase your income by more than it costs you. If you are like most people, you spend most of your money on one thing or another in an attempt to be happier. Vivation will work a lot better to make you happier than all that other stuff will. After a few sessions you will be able to use Vivation on your own without assistance and will not have to invest any more money. I suspect you'll find that Vivation is a better value for your money than anything else in the world!

Some Useful Questions to Ask When Choosing Your Vivation Professional

In your initial conversations with a prospective Vivation Professional, here are some questions I recommend asking:

1) How will you teach me to Vive?

2) Please tell me about your personal experience with Vivation.

3) Please tell me how you learned to be a Vivation Professional.

4) Please describe your approach to coaching sessions.

5) Please tell me all the services you make available.

Additionally, if you have something particular you want to work on in your sessions, you can ask "What has been your experience of working with people who ____ ?"

What Vivation Sessions Might Be Like For You

You will have your own unique experience with Vivation, substantially different from the experience of anyone else and substantially different from what I tell you here. In this section I am going to attempt to explain a few kinds of experiences that occur frequently.

You will probably meet your Vivation Professional for the first time when you go to his or her office to get your first session. The first few minutes might simply be getting to know one another, a chance for both of you to ask each other a few questions and become comfortable with each other.

Your Vivation Professional will then begin teaching you the internal skills. There are several different ways to do this. Some Vivation Professionals teach The Three Points to Remember in the first session, leading you through a series of experiential exercises. Other Vivation Professionals prefer to spend a little time on each one of The Five Elements, also with experiential exercises and probably with explanations, as well.

All Vivation Professionals teach Circular Breathing in the first session. This will probably involve a demonstration by the Vivation Professional and a chance for you to try it. Depending on various factors, you might learn a lot of detail about the breathing in your first session, or just the basics.

The educational part of your first session will probably take about one hour. Like everything else about Vivation, this could be either longer or shorter depending on you and your Vivation Professional. Your Vivation Professional will make sure that you understand enough to embark on what could be the most amazing experience of your life.

The Vivation Session

After a short break you will position yourself comfortably, either lying down or sitting. You will close your eyes. Your Vivation Professional will offer you suggestions, probably recommending that you begin with some slow full Circular Breathing.

The first few minutes of your first session will probably involve getting used to the breathing and the enhanced energy-flow in your body. Some people are very surprised when they start feeling the energy, others less so. Some people experience some initial difficulty with the breathing, other people find it comfortable and natural from the very beginning. Your Vivation Professional remembers vividly his or her first time, and will be sensitive to your needs.

Within a few minutes, patterns of energy will start emerging and the Vivation Professional will guide you into exploring and integrating these. The patterns of energy could be like anything! They might seem familiar or they might seem totally weird. Words fail to describe this experience, but we use words anyway. Your first pattern of energy could feel like an emotion, sadness for example. It could be like sleepiness. It could be an itching sensation, or a tingling sensation. You might suddenly start feeling very warm or cold. Some physical pain in your body might start to stand out more than usual. Or you might not have any of that, and your Vivation Professional will simply guide you into focusing on ordinary physical sensations in your body, to help you open your feeling awareness.

Sometimes in the first session, one feeling comes up early and lasts for the entire session. More often, the feeling that comes up first will only last for a few minutes before it integrates. Integration feels different at different times. Sometimes integrations are very dramatic, with a huge release of energy and an astonishing insight or outburst of laughter. Other times they are very subtle and it will only seem like some other feeling starts to predominate. Do not concern yourself with whether or not you have integrated, but instead just keep focusing on whatever feeling is strongest in the present moment.

The next feeling that comes up might seem related to the first one or it might seem completely different. Again, don't worry about that, just keep Viving. During the course of your session, many, many different feelings might come up and move all around your body.

During your session, your Vivation Professional will also be Viving, having his or her own experiences while coaching you. Sometimes you might hear your Vivation Professional's breathing. Viving while coaching you is the proper thing for your coach to do. In fact we have a saying in Vivation, "The best way to give your Viver an excellent session is to give yourself an even better session."

Your Vivation Professional observes you very closely during your session, watching, listening, sensing. Sometimes your Vivation Professional will know what you are experiencing in surprising detail, and other times not. Your Vivation Professional does not need to know the content of your experience in order to coach you, but only how you are responding to your experience. All he or she needs to know is whether you are staying in all Five Elements, and which one of the five is weakest for you at the moment. Every few minutes your Vivation Professional might say something to you, to help you stay in The Five Elements. These suggestions might be for a change in the breathing rhythm, a reminder to focus your attention on your feeling awareness, a Fourth Element technique, or something else. Many Vivation Professionals offer one of The Three Points to Remember as a suggestion every few minutes no matter what. Throughout your session you will always be able to talk with your Vivation Professional to share something or ask something, although most of the time you will do better to just keep Viving instead of talking. The suggestions your Vivation Professional offers you are only suggestions, and you can always choose to follow the advice or not, although usually you will get the best results by taking his or her suggestions.

As the session progresses, you will experience layer after layer of suppression disappearing. You will begin to get a feeling of the vastness of yourself, and to view this vastness with reverence and humility.

Completion

Whatever has been interfering with your ability to fully enjoy your aliveness comes to your attention, feeling-by-feeling, and is transformed, integrated. After some period of time, usually from one to two hours, you will reach the point of completion for the session—the magical moment when there is no more block against enjoyment and you feel the profound joy of aliveness itself.

Every session has its own natural point of completion, when everything has been integrated. Generally you will do better to keep Viving until you reach this point, and not end your session according to a clock. You might think you are complete for your session before your Vivation Professional thinks so. Trust the experience of your Vivation Professional. You will get better results from your session if you go all the way through to completion.

Your session is complete when all of the following criteria are met:

1. A satisfactory amount of suppressed material came up and was integrated.

2. Everything that was activated was integrated. (This simply means that you, the Viver, feel wonderful.)

3. Both you and your Vivation Professional agree that the first two criteria were met.

If you are feeling disorientated or uncomfortable then your session is not yet complete. Keep Viving!

If you are feeling good, energized, and relaxed, then your session is complete.

A peculiar paradox about completion is that when you feel like you could happily keep Viving forever, then your session is complete. When you feel an urge to stop, then your session is not complete.

When your session is complete, you will have the opportunity to talk with your Vivation Professional about your session. Your Vivation Professional might give you a homework assignment to complete before your next appointment. This homework may or may not include trying some self-Vivation before you come back next time.

Scheduling Sessions

Most people like to get Vivation sessions once a week, although you might prefer either more often or less often. Most people like to have their appointments at the same time on the same day of the week each time, but that may not be good for you for some reason. I recommend that you not go more than three weeks between sessions, because if you do, you will start to get out of practice with the internal skill and you will have a harder time learning to master the process.

When you go for your second session you will probably expect it to be something like your first session, but it won't be. No two sessions will ever be alike because once you integrate something it won't come up in your sessions again. Each pattern of energy feels quite different to Vive into. The range of feelings that comes up in Vivation is absolutely astonishing!

Almost everyone integrates a lot of material in the first session and then integrates more and more material faster and faster as the sessions progress. Every session will begin with a lesson to help you to further develop your skill with the process. At the end of each session you will probably feel better than you ever did before.

Unconsciousness

Sometime during the course of your sessions you will probably go through a period of unconsciousness, in which you feel very sleepy. This might happen in your first few sessions, or maybe not until later. Many different things can cause this unconsciousness. You don't need to know what is causing it in order to integrate it. When you are experiencing unconsciousness, do not Vive lying down. Either sit up or stand up. Breathe fast and fully. Focus on the exact physical sensations that the sleepiness is producing in your body. Embrace that feeling just like you embrace other feelings. The unconsciousness does not indicate that you are doing something wrong. The unconsciousness itself is an extremely important pattern of energy. Welcome it!

Everybody has some suppressed shame. Shame consists of your negative contexts about yourself. When shame comes up in Vivation sessions, it usually appears initially as unconsciousness. Shame integrates just like any other feelings do, by feeling it in detail and embracing it. Don't believe your shame when it comes up, but rather keep Viving into it. Integration of your shame will make your entire life look very much better to you.

Pleasure Tolerance

Pleasure tolerance is a topic that needs to be addressed by all personal growth methodologies. Pleasure tolerance means only being able to accept life as pleasurable up to some limit. It means not allowing your life to get *too* good. Pleasure tolerance is created by shame, negative conditioning from religion, seeing unhappy adults as role models when you were a child, and other sources. Anything you do that improves your life will activate your pleasure tolerance. For example, if you learn how to increase your income, you will either have to accept having life be more pleasurable than you thought it should be, make certain you don't allow yourself to enjoy your wealth too much, or sabotage your efforts. Obviously the first of these options is the most desirable.

In order to get the most benefit from any program of personal development, you need to directly challenge your pleasure tolerance. Do this by focusing on the pleasure of pleasurable experiences and taking in the pleasure as consciously as you can. Vivation itself directly challenges the pleasure tolerance by giving you concentrated practice at enjoying each moment of your life.

In general, whatever gets integrated in a completed Vivation session stays integrated forever, although make-wrong is an eternal option that goes with having a mind. Nonetheless, not all your make-wrongs will get integrated in one session or even in several sessions. The bad news is that, if you are like most normal human beings, you have thousands of make-wrongs suppressed in your unconscious mind. The good news is two-fold: 1) every integration feels wonderful; and, 2) every integration makes the next integration easier.

Number of Assisted Sessions

I recommend that you get at least ten sessions from the same Vivation Professional. This does not necessarily have to be the person you started with, if you have some good reason to switch. But do get ten sessions from one person.

The reason for ten sessions is that it is enough for you to get a good idea of what the process is and how it applies to various types of suppressed material. The reason for doing them with one person is that one person will get to know you well and, for that reason, will be much better at facilitating and educating you. Also you will know that the differences from session to session come from you. If you are constantly changing Vivation Professionals, you will partly think that the differences from session to session come from them.

Different Formats of Vivation

As you progress through sessions, your Vivation Professional might suggest trying Vivation sessions in special formats, which might include warm water sessions, cold water sessions, Vivation in Action, and so on. I will say a little about each one.

Warm Water Vivation

Vivation in warm water is good because warm water accelerates activation of suppressed material. If a person is skillful at integrating, this accelerated activation is advantageous because even more can be accomplished in the same amount of time. Additionally, everyone has suppressed important feelings related to their own birth. Warm water Vivation supports the activation of these feelings.

Warm water Vivation is done in a natural hot spring, large bathtub or other pool of water where the water temperature can be maintained just above body temperature at 98°-102° F (38°-39° C) and in which the Viver has enough room to be comfortable. There are several good ways to do this, but the best is for the Viver to have a good quality snorkel to breathe through while immersed, face down in the warm water.

Cold Water Vivation

For most people, cold water Vivation is even more activating than warm water Vivation. One explanation for this is that warm water speeds activation by adding energy to your energy system from the outside, while cold water speeds activation by requiring your body to increase its own energy from the inside. The biological process by which your body keeps you warm is called thermogenesis. Thermogenesis increases the energy flow in your body in somewhat the same way that full breathing does. The cold water may also activate feelings related to death. Cold water Vivation is an appropriate step after the Viver has gained confidence with warm water Vivation.

Cold water Vivation is done in water that feels cool or cold to the touch, generally below 80° F (25° C). I know some Vivation Professionals whom I respect a lot who routinely do cold water sessions in water very near freezing. I have done Vivation in water of this temperature and have known many other people who have also done so. However, I recommend not going below 60° F (15° C). Fast and full Circular Breathing makes it possible to Vive in water colder than you would expect, without going into hypothermia. Even so, at temperatures that are too cold, the cold itself becomes the point of the session, which is not really what you want. In water of 70° F (20° C), which is about the right temperature for the majority of people, the emotions are the main point. Your mind might tell you that you feel uncomfortable because of the cold, but really the context is the culprit.

Cold water Vivation, once you master it, is an incredibly invigorating experience. The increased energy lasts for a substantial period after you get out of the water.

Vivation in Action

Vivation in Action means Viving while you are engaging simultaneously in another activity: public speaking, driving your car, hiking in the woods, and so on. You can Vive while engaging in any activity, provided you are good enough at Vivation. Since the events of daily life can be emotionally activating, you will want to master Vivation in Action. Ultimately your goal will be to Vive continuously.

A Vivation in Action adventure means Viving while you do something that you know will activate your emotions. Here are some examples of Vivation in Action adventures: Viving on a roller-coaster, Viving while sky-diving, Viving while selling a product or service to a customer, Viving while dancing, Viving while house-cleaning, and many others. Vivation in Action Adventures not only enable you to integrate feelings that have always limited you in the past, they can also be immensely entertaining!

Eyegaze Vivation

Eyegaze Vivation is done by having two people sit across from one another, Viving while maintaining eye contact. Group Eyegaze Vivation is Viving with many people sitting in a circle, Viving with eye contact. A remarkable sense of "merging" is often experienced. Although people sometimes feel apprehensive about Eyegaze Vivation before they try it, people invariably become comfortable with it within minutes. For many people, including me, this is the most powerful form of Vivation. Group Eyegaze Vivation is a featured part of all my seminars and trainings.

Mirror Vivation

Mirror Vivation is Viving while maintaining eye contact with yourself in a mirror. This is extremely powerful, for several reasons. You can often see emotions on your face even before feeling them. Your emotions related to self-esteem come up strongly. You might even see your own spirit! For some people, Mirror Vivation is more activating than either warm water or cold water Vivation. Even if you are very experienced at Vivation, I suggest having a coach with you the first time you try this, because it can be more activating than you expect.

Vivation Autonomy

Vivation autonomy means taking complete responsibility for your own on-going Vivation process. This means taking responsibility for your results even when you are being coached. It also means learning to do Vivation without your Vivation Professional. Vivation Autonomy means doing everything necessary to master the process.

Vivation is a self-help process. Only you can produce the results of Vivation for yourself. Until you have had several Vivation sessions, you will probably be unable to give yourself a complete Vivation session without your Vivation Professional coaching you. To get the maximum results from Vivation you will ultimately have to break that dependency.

Vivation autonomy means admitting the truth when you do need help. It means making sure you get the help you need. It means making sure you get coached sessions from someone (your Vivation Professional or someone else) even after you learn to do excellent self-Vivation. Vivation Autonomy means creating and maintaining a program that will further the development of your Vivation skills, help you to stay integrated, and continue to be interesting for you.

Buddy-System Vivation

Assisted Vivation sessions continue to be highly useful to people long after they develop the ability to Vive by themselves effectively. One of the most practical ways for advanced Vivation students to get assisted Vivation sessions on a regular basis is to trade Vivation sessions with another Vivation student. This has the obvious benefits of saving money and increasing your confidence with the process. During self-Vivation you function as both the coach and Viver, so any experience you get with coaching others will increase your ability to Vive by yourself. Trading Vivation sessions with your friend or spouse is known as "Buddy-system Vivation," and the person with whom you trade Vivation sessions is known as your "Vivation Buddy."

You and your Vivation Buddy need to have enough experience and knowledge to be competent at coaching each other. Additionally, you need to be able to keep your relationship with your Vivation Buddy fairly clear. This can be particularly tricky when your Vivation Buddy is your husband or wife. Essentially, what you need is to be able to tell each other the truth about everything, even when this is emotionally difficult.

Your Vivation Professional will help you learn to trade sessions with your Vivation Buddy. Some Vivation Professionals provide special sessions in which you and your Vivation Buddy take turns coaching each other while your Vivation Professional supervises and writes copious notes to the coach in the pair.

Buddy-System Vivation is an important step on the road to Vivation autonomy.

Self-Vivation

Your goal should be to become competent at producing the results of Vivation by yourself. If you have not yet developed that ability at the end of ten sessions with your Vivation Professional, then get more sessions. Some people learn to do self-Vivation faster and some learn to do it slower. I generally tell people to expect to need between five and fifteen sessions to learn to do consistently excellent self-Vivation. Everyone can learn self-Vivation and every Vivation Professional is committed to teaching you how to do self-Vivation. Many Vivation Professionals routinely have their Vivers start trying self-Vivation after their first session, provided the Viver has no major discomfort or problems during the first session.

Even when you are very happy going to your Vivation Professional for sessions, you still need to learn self-Vivation. There are two very important reasons for this. The more obvious reason is that you simply cannot have your Vivation Professional with you all the time. If you get upset about something, you don't want to wait until you can get a session with your Vivation Professional. The less obvious reason is even more important. Some feelings, especially those related to loneliness, will come up more readily for you when you are by yourself than when you are with your Vivation Professional. Integrating these feelings of loneliness is essential to developing autonomy, not only with Vivation, but in life in general.

Vivation Professional Trainings

The most experienced and knowledgeable Vivation Professionals lead Vivation Professional Trainings from time to time. These are offered in various formats and are very reasonably priced considering the wealth of information they contain. If you are interested in a career as a Vivation Professional, then obviously you will need to take Trainings. But even if you have no interest in teaching Vivation to other people, I highly recommend these Trainings to you for several reasons: 1) You will learn a great deal that will make you better at producing the results of Vivation for yourself; 2) You will have excellent

Vivation sessions during the training; 3) You will meet people at the Training that you can trade sessions with, and develop the skills you need to be able to trade sessions well; 4) You will have a very enjoyable experience from which you will receive life-long benefit.

The Importance of Your Vivation Community

Many, many people are using Vivation nowadays. When you learn Vivation, you are not alone. However, when you do Vivation you will experience things that most of your friends, family, and co-workers have not experienced. Some examples: You will feel your body as an energy system. You will feel your breathing make a gigantic difference in how you feel. You will feel emotions emerge from suppression and integrate into bliss. You will discover that you can change your relationship to something unpleasant in a way that allows it to become pleasant. You will have direct contact with your own individual spirit. If you are like most people, you will want to be able to discuss some of these things with other people who have also experienced them. Additionally, you may find some aspects of developing skill with Vivation difficult at first, and you may want to talk with other people who had these difficulties when they were starting, and succeeded in overcoming them. For these reasons, and others, you will do well to have contact with other people in your community who are also doing Vivation.

Most Vivation Professionals do their best to make it easy for their clients to participate in the local Vivation

Community. There are various ways they do this. Some Vivation Professionals conduct Eyegaze Vivation groups on a weekly basis. Some have on-going classes. Some hold parties, or organize other kinds of social events with members of the Vivation Community. I suggest that you tell your Vivation Professional that you would like to be an active participant in your local Vivation Community. I also suggest that you take a share of the responsibility for helping to maintain your local community, and ask your Vivation Professional what you can do to contribute. You will get the most benefit from your Vivation Community if you take an active role.

Developing Your Personal Vivation Program

Develop your own personal program for getting the most benefit from your skill with Vivation. Design your individual program to fit your own personal needs. Here are some ideas that work well:

Do your best to Vive continuously, but be patient with yourself when you forget or suppress.

Do some Vivation every day, even if it's only five minutes.

Put up signs around your house, car, work place, and so on, reminding yourself of The Five Elements and The Three Points to Remember.

Make a practice of always Viving while you do some of your daily activities, such as bathing, washing the dishes, etc.

After you get ten sessions from one Vivation Professional, try getting some sessions from some other Vivation Professionals. You will learn something new from each person.

Be certain to have a minimum of one absolutely complete Vivation session every three weeks. Once a week is preferable, but if you go more than three weeks, you'll get out of practice.

In self-Vivation, expect loneliness to come up. Welcome it—loneliness integrates the same as anything else.

Include some mirror Vivation, some warm water Vivation and some cold water Vivation in your regular practice.

Avoid indulging "urgency patterns" that come up during self-Vivation. Urgency patterns are when the activation of a feeling gives you a huge desire to go do something immediately, without completing your session first. There are various kinds of urgency patterns. Sometimes you may have a great idea, and want to go take immediate action on the idea. Sometimes you may feel anger getting activated, and want to get on the phone and yell at someone. Sometimes you may feel a huge desire to go eat some cake or drink some wine. No matter what urgency patterns come up, complete your session first, then take action, if you still want to.

If self-Vivation isn't producing the results you desire, for any reason, then get a coached session immediately from a Vivation Professional or Vivation Buddy.

Learn to coach sessions. Trade sessions with other experienced Vivers as often as you can. Your personal practice will benefit enormously from coaching other people through sessions. If you live in a place where there are no other people doing Vivation, you can take a Professional Training and then come home and teach someone else. Then you'll have someone to trade with.

Do Vivation in Action in public places. Until you do this, your mind will tell you that everyone is going to think you are noticeably weird if you Vive at the market, in church, on the bus, and so on. If you listen to your mind when it tells you it's weird to Vive in public, then you'll try to be just as suppressed as everybody else! In actual practice, people will not notice anything about you when you are Viving in public, except that you may seem particularly friendly and alive. Some people will have a lot better day because of some casual contact with you when you are Viving in public. The only way you'll find out about this for yourself is by doing it. The first time you Vive in public may seem awkward, but just do it anyway. The only way you can get maximum benefit from Vivation in Action is to learn to do it in the presence of other people.

As much as possible, surround yourself with others who Vive.

Learn to include your feelings in what you're doing. Most people find that, at first, they can do Vivation in Action more effectively while engaging in physical activities, rather than mental ones. With practice, however, you will find that you can do Vivation in Action while programming a computer, writing a book, etc.

Take yourself on courageous Vivation in Action Adventures. Think about the situations you have learned to avoid because they activate your emotions too much. Speaking in public, going to church, and talking to your father-in-law might be a few examples. Then do those things intentionally for the purpose of activating your emotions, and keep Viving while you do them!

Learn to identify make-wrong and tell yourself the truth about it when you're doing it. In other words, don't believe your mind when your mind tells you that someone or something is responsible for your upset. Acknowledge that reality must be perfect as it is, and your upset must be your responsibility.

Avoid agreeing with others when they are making something wrong. This doesn't mean you have to argue with them. Just think to yourself, "It's perfect that this person thinks this way about things, and I am grateful that I don't!" Or, "This person may be right about this thing being wrong, but I am sure grateful that it's not worse!"

Take some Vivation seminars, led by very experienced Vivation Professionals. You will probably find that people who have led many seminars, over a period of years, have interesting perspectives about things.

Take Vivation breaks during the day. These can be as simple as just doing the "Breathing Range Exercise," described in Chapter 4. That will take less than five minutes. If you do have the time, then do a Vivation session for a few minutes longer.

An excellent idea is to do Vivation as a meditation, and make a practice of doing two twenty-minute sessions every day, one in the morning and the other in the afternoon or evening.

If you live or work with someone else who is exerienced at Vivation, you can give each other short, coached mini-sessions, particularly when one of you is having an especially difficult day. What sometimes happens for me is that on days when I feel really frustrated I also feel really pressured to keep working. On such days I would usually feel that I could not take the time for a complete Vivation session, but I can always accept that a fifteen break might increase, rather than decrease my productivity. On such days a coach can be really helpful in making a short session effective.

Avoid suppressive activities. Avoid excessive drinking, drug-taking, TV-watching, and other activities that tend to take your awareness away from your feelings. Suppressive bad habits can make it much harder to do self-Vivation and Vivation in Action.

During your Vivation sessions, only do Vivation. Pay close attention to what I'm telling you here: It's a great idea to do Vivation while you do something else, but it's a bad idea to do something else *during your Vivation session.* For example, if you are getting a massage, you'll get an even better result if you Vive at the same time. But if you get massaged during your Vivation session, you won't notice that you can produce all of your own results from the inside. An increase in autonomy is a major benefit that you want to receive every time you do a

Vivation session. Very often when people are trained to become Vivation Professionals, they already know how to do some sort of healing technique on people. They have to be sure to keep the techniques separate by not doing healing techniques on clients during their Vivation sessions.

Continuously monitor yourself and everyone around you, to see which of The Five Elements is weakest at the moment. This will help you to strengthen your own application of The Five Elements.

Begin to think of Vivation as a necessary part of maintaining your body, just like eating, sleeping and exercising. Don't wait for your emotions to get so strong that you have to Vive.

Spend time in nature regularly. By observing nature outside your body, you can learn a great deal about nature inside your body.

Take the best care of your health that you can. While it is true that Vivation works starting from any condition of mind or body, it is also true that it is easier to Vive if you are in a good state of health. If you are ill, your illness will provide the main patterns of energy in your body and you will spend your Vivation time mainly focusing on these. This can be excellent for easing the discomfort and speeding the healing of the illness, but it reduces your ability to experience the subtler patterns of energy.

Become aware of the planet and our relationship with it. In particular, I think every Vivation Professional should participate actively in the movement to improve air quality. Air pollution makes it harder to get benefits from

Vivation. Air pollution is directly contrary to the interests of people who Vive. Become very insistent that your government and other institutions do everything practicable to improve the quality of air, both outside and indoors. You do make a difference.

Be courageous and go for it! Take responsibility for your own feelings and actions and dare to lead the way for global liberation. Be gentle on yourself when things look "bad" and remember to have the same compassion for yourself as you would have for your best friend. Love yourself even when you are activated. Share your love with the planet.

ABOUT THE AUTHOR

Jim Leonard developed the Vivation process, including The Five Elements of Vivation, in 1979. His first book, *Vivation* was published in 1983, and was subsequently translated into eight languages. His second book, *Your Fondest Dream*, which is about practical applications of creativity, came out in 1989, and is also available in French and Spanish.

During his life-long investigation of personal growth methods, he has studied hatha yoga, kundalini yoga, Taoist methods, shamanism, Buddhism, Hinduism, mystic Christianity, and rebirthing. In 1980 he was ordained as a Healing Minister in the Eastern Orthodox Church (Malabar Rite).

From 1985 to 1992, he traveled constantly, teaching a seminar somewhere almost every weekend. He has personally coached more than 30,000 Vivation sessions in twenty countries. Nowadays he prefers to travel somewhat less, although he still makes three seminar tours to Europe each year.

In 1987 he founded Associated Vivation Professionals (AVP), the worldwide professional organization of Vivation, providing a referral service as well as other services for Vivation Professionals and the public. Jim has taught hundreds of people to have a rewarding career as a Vivation Professional.

Beginning in 1990, Jim researched simpler methods for teaching Vivation. This work culminated, in 1993, in The Three Points to Remember. The Three Points to Remember make Vivation so easy to do that even little children learn it easily.

In 1995, Jim was appointed a professor at Loja University in Turin, Italy, teaching Vivation as part of the world's first fully accredited graduate program in the field of personal growth.

In addition to his hundreds of seminars for the public, Jim has also taught seminars on applied creativity for companies both large and small.

Jim lives in Palm Beach, Florida, with Lans, Kyra, Apollo and Mystic.

Associated Vivation Professionals (AVP)

Associated Vivation Professionals (AVP) is a worldwide professional organization of people dedicating their lives to making Vivation available to the public. AVP will provide you a list of Vivation Professionals in your area, let you know about upcoming seminars, and provide you with other literature and services that you will find helpful. Here is where to contact AVP:

Associated Vivation Professionals
PO Box 2595
Minneapolis, MN 55402

From the United States or Canada, phone TOLL FREE:

1-800-829-2625

From outside the USA and Canada, phone:

001-612-377-VIVE

Listing of Vivation Professionals

(as of 3/1/96)

David N. Alexander, AVP
5827 Nicollet Avenue South
Minneapolis, MN 55419
(612) 861-3219
(612) 996-5487 (24-hour voicemail)

Elvira Cruz Armendariz, MSW, AVP
Life Enrichment Services
PO Box 6497
McAllen, Texas 78502-6497
(210) 519-8065

White Ash, AVP
Director of AVP USA/Canada
P.O. Box 2595
Minneapolis, MN 55402
(612) 377-VIVE! (24-hour)

White Ash attended professional trainings with Jim Leonard and Lans Peterson in '93 and '94, has been a breathwork student and practitioner since '91, and is offering the gamut of Vivation experiences for you today!

Patricia Bacall
3435 Ocean Park Blvd. #112
Santa Monica, CA 90405
(310) 441-5445 or (500) 44-PATTI

Carla Cohen
Redondo Beach, CA
(310)540-6640
Personal Effectiveness Consultant - Specializing in personal growth for over twelve years. I am a Seminar Leader, Bodyworker and Vivation® Professional Trainer. In addition to breath work, I offer powerful and gentle body work, specializing in effective Body Language through tissue communication (I have apprenticed with Patrick Collard and am a Body Harmony® Practioner). If you're committed to surpassing your limitations call for an appointment.

Anthony Dallmann-Jones, Ph.D. AVP Board Member
Author, *PHOENIX FLIGHT MANUAL...Rising Above the Ashes of Ordinary Existence,* and
RESOLVING UNFINISHED BUSINESS...The Effects of Being Raised in a Dysfunctional Environment
"I conduct workshops and seminars in personal empowerment where you are, or you can stay with me for personal training. One of my specialties is quickly moving people and organizations from their trauma history into their fully manifested potential. Call."
PO Box 1181 Fond du Lac, WI 54936-1181 USA
Telephone: (414)921-6991 Fax:414-921-7691
asdjones@wis.com Web site:*http://didley.com/wolfcreek*

StevenFarmer
Laguna Beach, CA
(714) 494-2544

Robert Hesketh
P.O.Box 2258
London, England W1A 1YU

Chad Klapes
PO Box 51
Housatonic, MN 01236
(413) 274-3375   800-806-8193

Gloria Krause
Thousand Oaks, CA USA
(805) 497-1712

Lee Kuntz & Letty Anne Martin
3627 Keystone Avenue #2
Los Angeles, CA 90034
(310) 839-4378

Jill Robinson, BA, CQSW, CMS
VIVATION PROFESSIONAL
56 Windermere Road
LANCASTER LA1 3EZ
LANCASHIRE ENGLAND
TEL: 01524-64183

Wally Wallin
Stockton, CA USA
(209) 941-4440

Study VIVATION with JIM LEONARD!

You can learn Vivation, either as a novice or an advanced student, directly with the originator of the Vivation Process. You can study Vivation in any of several formats: The Vivation Professional Training, weekend seminars, small groups ("shared sessions") or private sessions. You can profit from producing a weekend seminar in your area, for the benefit of your community. Also your company can have a seminar in applied creativity, custom-designed for its special needs.

THE VIVATION PROFESSIONAL TRAINING

The Vivation Professional Training includes everything you need to start a successful career as a Vivation Professional. Typically, about half the people who take the Training do so to develop a career and the other half take it for the intensive personal growth experience.

The Training is very thorough. It covers the bet methods for succeeding in your own business and making your work as blissful as your sessions.

Each participant receives seven assisted Vivation sessions, and gives eight sessions, including one to someone who has never experienced Vivation before. The sessions include experience in both warm and cold water.

Weekend Seminars with JIM LEONARD

Weekend seminars are an excellent way to get started in Vivation or to develop your Vivation skills more fully. Seminars are available on a variety of topics, all including extensive experience with the Vivation process.

For a schedule of events and further information about any of Jim Leonard's services, phone, write or email:

Jim Leonard
PO Box 2384
Palm Beach, FL 33480 USA
407-588-6833
Internet: 73632,3366@compuserve.com

~~~~~~

LANS PETERSON

VIVATION Sessions and Seminars

LANS PETERSON is known worldwide as a seminar leader and Vivation Trainer. She has taught Vivation in 15 countries. For over 20 years she has been a student and teacher of meditation, shamanism, and natural healing. Lans is the International Coordinator of Associated Vivation Professionals (AVP) and was the Director of AVP for the United States and Canada from 1992 until 1995. She is the Chair of the World Board of Trustees of AVP and serves as AVP's World Coordinator. Call or write:

Lans Peterson P.O. Box 2384 Palm Beach, FL 33480 USA
407-588-6833
~~~~~~

VIVATION® EN MEXICO

Aprende a ser más feliz a través de un proceso natural de respiración y relajación, observando y aceptando tu momento presente.

Sesiones individuales, talleres de fin de semana y de entrenamiento para instructores.

DIRECTORIO DE INSTRUCTORES DE VIVATION® EN MEXICO

Kurt Denker Tel (525)* 578-0618
Fax (525)* 588-0670 y 652-3148

Guadalupe Coello Tel (525)* 560-4698 y 308-2434

Virginia Luviano Tel/Fax (525)* 660-1477

VIVATION® y VIVATION ES LA HABILIDAD DE SER FELIZ® son marcas comerciales registradas en México por Kurt Denker Reese, y sólo pueden ser usadas en publicidad y promoción de servicios relacionados con la educación y el desarrollo humano por personas que obtengan la LICENCIA de derecho de uso correspondiente. El directorio solamente enlista los instructores de VIVATION® en México y el otorgante de licencias de derecho de uso de las marcas VIVATION® y VIVATION ES LA HABILIDAD DE SER FELIZ® no se responsabiliza de las actividades de los instructores enlistados.

VIVATION® es una marca registrada de servicio y una marca registrada editorial de Jim Leonard bajo nombre comercial ASSOCIATED VIVATION® PROFESSIONALS. La habilidad de VIVATION® fue creada por Jim Leonard.

* (525) es unicamente para llamadas desde los Estados Unidos.

NETWORK DE PROSPERIDAD® EN MEXICO

Conoce tu propósito en la vida y realízalo en un trabajo placentero. Aprovecha la abundancia de tus recursos internos en todas las áreas de tu vida.

El objetivo del Network de Prosperidad® es crear y difundir la CONCIENCIA DE PROSPERIDAD® en México y el mundo. Las enseñanzas están respaldadas por el libro de Phil Laut "El dinero es mi amigo" cuyo propósito es eliminar la pobreza del mundo.

Si te interesa participar en la enseñanza de los conceptos de UNA NUEVA CONCIENCA DE PROSPERIDAD® como instructor, puedes obtener tu licencia de derecho de uso de nuestras siete marcas registradas, para fines publicitarios relacionados con el desarrollo humnaó.

Talleres de fin de semana; cursos intermedios de 8 a 10 sesiones y cursos de 1 año.

Puedes obtener informacion adicional acerca de los temas de VIVATION® y CONCIENCA DE PROSPERIDAD® comunicándote en México con:

Kurt Denker - Apartado postal 7-1243, 06700 México, D.F.
Tel (525)* 578-0618 Fax (525)* 588-0670 y 652-3148

* (525) es unicamente para llamadas desde los Estados Unidos.

Other THREE BLUE HERONS Products

PHOENIX FLIGHT MANUAL...Rising Above The Ashes of Ordinary Existence by Anthony S. Dallmann-Jones, Ph.D. A major contribution to the self-help field, wherein the latest quantum physical and psychological science is translated into easily applied everyday language. Includes case studies of people who have used the Phoenix Solution to lose weight, lower golf scores, reduce stress, cure illness, solve relationship problems, and change moods at will. The ultimate book for those interested in true empowerment. (208 pp. paperback ISBN# 1-881952-49-5) Only $14.95!

RESOLVING UNFINISHED BUSINESS...Assessing the Effects of Being Raised in a Dysfunctional Environment by Anthony S. Dallmann-Jones, Ph.D. Are you clear on the aftereffects of being raised dysfunctionally with abuse and/or neglect? This book explains the eight characteristics that are leftovers in adults from a traumatic childhood, and how they influence schools, relationships, and the workplace. Includes self-assessing questionnaires and the first nomenclature of abuse and neglect. (176 pp. paperback ISBN# 1-881952-26-6) Only $12.95

ASSESSMENT FORMS -
If you are a teacher, social worker, mental or medical health worker, counselor, judicial system professional, or educator, and you truly want to understand your clients, nothing provides a clearer picture of an abuse/neglect history than CSCAN (for assessing children) or CSANA (for assessing adults). Each sheet includes all CSCAN or CSANA categories in a checklist format. Specify which you are ordering. (Samples upon request.)
Classification System for Child Abuse & Neglect **(CSCAN)**
Classification System for Abuse & Neglect in Adults **(CSANA)**
25 sheets per each 8.5 x 11 color-coded pad - Only $9.95 each

Note: All products are fully guaranteed for the cost of the item(s).

THREE BLUE HERONS PUBLISHING, INC.
303 Gillett Street Fond du Lac, WI 54935 USA 800-665-0755

Order Form

Name______________________________Tel______
Address____________________________________
City&State___________________________Zip_____

___Copies of *The Skill of Happiness* @ $12.95= ______
___Copies of *Phoenix Flight Manual*@ $14.95= ______
___Copies of *Resolving Unfinished Business*
@ $12.95= ______
___CSCAN (child) Assessment pads @ $9.95= ______
___CSANA (adult) Assessment pads @ $9.95= ______

(Wisc. residents add 5% sales tax to mdse. price) ______

Add shipping: $5 for the first item and $1 for each additional item: ______

TOTAL:________

Allow 3 weeks for delivery. Satisfaction guaranteed for amount of purchase.

Mail ORDER FORM along with check/money
or purchase order #__________ to:

Three Blue Herons Publishing, Inc.
P. O. Box 463 Fond du Lac, WI 54936-0463 USA

Resellers call 3BH for rates & terms: 414/921-6991